Egyptian Mau Cats

A Complete Owner's Guide

Published By ROC Publishing 2014

Copyright and Trademarks

This publication is Copyright 2014 by ROC Publishing. All products, publications, software and services mentioned and recommended in this publication are protected by trademarks. In such instance, all trademarks & copyright belong to the respective owners. All rights reserved. No part of this book may be reproduced or transferred in any form or by any means, graphic, electronic, or mechanical including photocopying, recording, taping, or by any information storage retrieval system, without the written permission of the author. Pictures used in this book are either royalty free pictures bought from stock-photo websites or have the source mentioned underneath the picture.

Disclaimer and Legal Notice

This product is not legal or medical advice and should not be interpreted in that manner. You need to do your own due-diligence to determine if the content of this product is right for you. The author and the affiliates of this product are not liable for any damages or losses associated with the content of this product. While every attempt has been made to verify the information shared in this publication, neither the author nor the affiliates assume any responsibility for errors, omissions or contrary interpretation of the subject matter herein. Any perceived slights to any specific person(s) or organization(s) are purely unintentional.

We have no control over the nature, content and availability of the web sites listed in this book. The inclusion of any website links does not necessarily imply a recommendation or endorse the views expressed within them. ROC Publishing takes no responsibility for, and will not be liable for, the websites being temporarily unavailable or being removed from the Internet.

The accuracy and completeness of information provided herein are not guaranteed or warranted to produce any particular results, and the advice and strategies, contained herein may not be suitable for every individual.

The author shall not be liable for any loss incurred as a consequence of the use and application, directly or indirectly, of any information presented in this work.

The publication is designed to provide information in regards to the subject matter covered.

Foreword

After a lifetime of being a cat owner, I didn't expect a breed to surprise me. Then I adopted an Egyptian Mau. Although Maus are completely domestic cats, the "wild" spotted appearance of these exceptionally lovely cats was the initial draw for me.

Then Heidi moved in and I began to experience feline companionship at a whole new level. She follows me everywhere I go, offering gentle commentary on the project at hand, and happily comes when I call her name.

One day, completely by accident, I held up a hoop, the sort you use to do needlework. With absolutely no prompting from me, Heidi jumped through it. I didn't even realize she was in the room!

Of course, I was delighted and invited her to do it again. She took a big running jump and sailed right through. When I laughed, she fairly beamed.

Egyptian Maus love to please their humans and I believe they have a sense of humor, or at least Heidi does. She'll always go for the laugh if she can get it.

The hoop trick has now evolved to diving leaps through an extendable cat tunnel. It's her favorite game after fetching wadded up balls of paper.

Sometimes she takes the grocery receipt out of the sack and will play with it in the middle of the kitchen floor as if it's

Foreword

the best cat toy ever! She's inventive and self-entertaining, while still craving my company.

Although I am very much an advocate of keeping cats indoors, I am lucky that in my current living circumstances, I can give her access to a secure portion of the back garden via a cat flap in the door.

It works wonderfully well – until she finds an interesting bamboo stick and tries to bring it inside for me to see! When I hear banging at the cat door, I know exactly what's happened.

What's even funnier though is how stubborn a Mau can be. More times than not, Heidi finds a way to snap the stick and get it inside no matter how stuck I think she may be.

All of life seems to fascinate her, and I am her most interesting project. She's quite sensitive to my moods and empathetic when I've had a bad day.

Unlike some Egyptian Maus that can be shy around strangers, Heidi likes to make friends with everyone who comes in the house.

She has shown no nervousness around other animals, and like many of her kind, is very fond of playing with water. In fact, she tipped her delicate little kitty bowl over so often, I finally gave in and bought her a massive dog bowl.

Often I find her experimentally swooshing the water around with her paw before taking a drink, and every

Foreword

morning she jumps in the shower as soon as I open the door to get out. She'll even sit on the edge of the tub and play in the water while I bathe.

To say that I have found her to be one of the most delightful cats I've ever known is something of an understatement. Heidi has made me a confirmed lover of Egyptian Maus, an affection I think you will instantly come to share if you find that this breed is a good fit for you and your household.

Foreword

Acknowledgements

Heidi-Pi – our *'pocco perro'*

Acknowledgements

Table of Contents

Foreword 1

Acknowledgements 5

Table of Contents 7

Chapter 1 – The Egyptian Mau 13

    Similarity to Other Spotted Species 14

        Savannah 14

        Chausie 15

        Serengeti 15

        Safari 16

    Egyptian Mau Physical Characteristics 16

        Size 17

        Coat and Colors 17

        Head, Eyes, and Ears 19

        Voice 20

        Reproduction 20

    The Egyptian Mau Personality 20

    Unique Behaviors 21

    With Children and Other Pets 23

    One Cat or Two? 24

Table of Contents

Male or Female 25

Egyptian Mau Clubs and Groups 26

Chapter 2 - Buying an Egyptian Mau Cat 29

Locating a Breeder 29

Conditions of Adoption 31

Mandatory Spaying and Neutering 31

Future Surrenders 32

Initial Health Evaluation 32

Lifestyle Inquiries 33

Your Questions for the Breeder 33

The Importance of Socialization 35

Judging a Kitten's Health 37

Adoption Paperwork 38

Declawing Expressly Forbidden 39

Genetic Health Conditions 39

Bringing Your Egyptian Mau 40

The Business of Kitten Proofing 41

The First Few Days 43

Approximate Costs 43

Chapter 3 – Daily Care Needs 46

Table of Contents

Feline Communication 101 47

Managing Your Cat's Diet 49

    Emphasize Quality Foods 50

    Selecting Appropriate Foods 54

    The Importance of Hydration 55

    Buying Food Bowls 56

Litter Box "Business" 57

    Considering Available Litters 59

    Picking a Litter Box 61

The Playful and Interactive Egyptian Mau 63

Scratching 65

Minimalist Mau Grooming 66

Chapter 4 – Health Care Facts 68

Attention to Routine Health Care 68

    Spaying and Neutering 69

    Recommended Vaccinations 71

    Understanding Feline Preventative Healthcare 73

Chapter 5 – Breeding and Showing 80

Deciding to Become a Breeder 80

    Factors to Consider 81

Table of Contents

Running the Numbers 83

Showing Egyptian Maus 85

    Proper Cat Show Attendance 87

    Cat Show Mechanics 89

Egyptian Mau Breed Standard 90

Chapter 6 – Egyptian Mau Cat Breeders 94

    Austria 94

    Canada 94

    Finland 95

    France 95

    Ireland 96

    Italy 96

    Netherlands 97

    Scotland 97

    United Kingdom 98

    United States 102

Afterword 106

Relevant Websites 108

Frequently Asked Questions 110

Glossary 116

Table of Contents

Index... 128

Table of Contents

Chapter 1 – The Egyptian Mau

You need only to go into the British Museum in London and gaze at the beautiful statues of the cat goddess Bastet to understand the relationship the ancient Egyptians had with domesticated felines.

More than 5,000 years ago, enterprising cats began a mutually beneficial association with the Egyptians, driving rats and snakes from the people's granaries and helping to stave off famine in the land.

For their service, the cats earned the respect of their human landlords. In time, the animals were not just seen as useful partners and beloved household companions, but also as sacred animals reputed to be the agents of the gods.

Chapter 1 – The Egyptian Mau

The spotted cats that existed in those days are believed to be the ancestors of the beautiful and modern Egyptian Mau, which makes this cat breed one of the oldest in the world.

Of course, there's no conclusive proof of this link, and the cats themselves aren't talking, but there is, without question, something inscrutable and ancient about this gorgeous breed.

The modern Egyptian Mau arrived in the United States in 1956 when three specimens were imported from Italy. The breed was granted championship status in 1968, and the International Cat Association recognized them in 1979. The cats remain relatively rare, however, with only a few thousand registered with the Cat Fanciers' Association.

Similarity to Other Spotted Species

It cannot be over-emphasized that the Egyptian Mau, although exotic in its appearance, is a completely domesticated breed with no wild blood. There are other spotted breeds that are much closer to their wild antecedents than the active, intelligent, and playful Mau.

Savannah

The Savannah, developed in the 1980s, represents a cross between an African Serval cat and a common domestic shorthair. Sometimes called a "house cheetah," Savannah are tall, slender cats with erect, alert ears. They can weigh as much as 20-30 lbs. (9-13 kg).

Chapter 1 – The Egyptian Mau

The breed has beautiful, dramatic spotting against a tawny background coat and is illegal in many locales in the F1-F3 generations. Typically F4 and later Savannahs are legal, but The International Cat Association (TICA) did not award the breed championship status until 2012.

Chausie

The Chausie is an elegant, gold cat with small, tight, black spotting. They are powerful athletes, renowned for their abilities at running and jumping.

The breed derives from selective pairing of Jungle Cats with domestic cats. The results are long-legged, graceful felines who are devoted, fearless, and very active.

Although the average size for a Chausie is 15 lbs. (6 kg), the breed can weigh up to 22 lbs. (9 kg).

Serengeti

Also a tawny, golden, dramatically spotted cat, the Serengeti is more "domestic" than other spotted breeds on purpose, with a lot of Bengal and oriental shorthair blood in the mix. The goal was to create a completely domestic cat with a strong resemblance to the African Serval.

The Serengeti is a medium-boned domestic cat with long legs, a short coat that is smooth and "tight," and distinctive black spotting.

Chapter 1 – The Egyptian Mau

Although not as large as some of the other spotted breeds, a male Serengeti will weigh 10-15 lbs. (4-6 kg), while females are only slightly smaller at 8-12 lbs. (3-5 kg).

Safari

In the 1970s, crosses of the South American Geoffroy's cat with domestic felines led to the creation of the rare hybrid Safari cat. Again the goal was a "wild" appearance, but these cats are extremely affectionate and social with their humans.

Unfortunately, the Safari is very difficult to breed because the foundation species do not have the same number of chromosomes. This makes for very uneven outcomes in pairings. A Safari can weigh a normal 8-12 lbs. (3-5 kg) or a whopping 25 lbs. (11 kg).

Egyptian Mau Physical Characteristics

Although completely domesticated, the Egyptian Mau has a gait reminiscent of the cheetah. A loose flap of skin running from their flanks to their hind legs gives them an unusually broad range of movement for executing twisting jumps that frankly don't seem possible until you've personally witnessed the acrobatic feat.

Often, these cats land on their back feet, which gives them an almost kangaroo-like appearance until they return to all fours. Maus have been clocked at top speeds of 30 mph / 48 kmh making them the fastest of all domestic cat breeds.

Chapter 1 – The Egyptian Mau

To look at an Egyptian Mau is to catch a glimpse of the exotic sleekness of a jungle creature. Refined, but with a suggestion of something wilder and more primitive, the Mau is a breathtaking beauty. No photograph can do justice to the depth of their glittering green eyes, or the gloss of their shiny spots.

There is a leopard-like elegance to their strong, graceful build. Because the hind legs are longer than the front, the Mau often appears to be tiptoeing as he walks.

Size

The Egyptian Mau is a medium-sized cat with a long body that should be extremely lithe in conformation. Their bodies have a pleasing, solid compactness that is a product of their sturdy musculature. Individuals will range from 6-14 lbs. /2.72-6.35 kg in weight.

Without question, the Mau is one of the superior athletes of the cat world, a fact you will soon discover when you welcome one into your home.

Coat and Colors

The Egyptian Mau is the only naturally spotted domestic cat. Their coat is short and silky with a gorgeous sheen. Accepted colors for the breed include silver, smoke, bronze, black and their dilutes -- blue silver, blue spotted, blue smoke, and blue.

Chapter 1 – The Egyptian Mau

Of these, the black and dilutes are not eligible to be shown in exhibitions, but they have all the excellent personality traits of the breed and are superb companions.

The spots must be clearly visible and not run together, but they may be of any size or shape to be acceptable for show.

There is a tabby "M" on the forehead as well as "frown lines," which run back between the ears and down the neck forming elongated spots along the backbone.

The spine itself is highlighted by a dark, dorsal stripe running from the head all the way to the tail.

Chapter 1 – The Egyptian Mau

Head, Eyes, and Ears

A Mau should have large "gooseberry" green eyes that are almond shaped and placed in perfect balance with the big, broad-based, and widely spaced ears.

The distinctive eye color may not be fully set until the cat is a year to a year and a half old. The coloration usually starts with a green ringing of the iris. In adults, the eyes have a tendency to flash from black to green when the animal is excited.

The breed exhibits a modified wedge shape to the head. The width of the distance between the eyes should be equal to the width at the end of the nose. This gives the Mau a look that has traditionally been described as "worried."

Voice

Gifted with a musical voice, Maus emit a delightful vocabulary of chortles and chirps. Conversational by nature, your Mau will offer up a considerable commentary on your life and actions, but without the slightly critical tone of the equally voluble Siamese.

This is one of the traits I enjoy most about the breed. I have always said that so long as I have a cat, I can never be accused of talking to myself. This is certainly true so long as I have a Mau in my life!

Reproduction

Egyptian Mau females have a longer gestation period than other domestic cat breeds. On average, a queen will carry her kittens for 63-67 days as opposed to the 58 common in others cats. Some females will go as long as 70 days, however, without exhibiting any problems at delivery.

The Egyptian Mau Personality

Egyptian Maus are exceptionally intelligent and display a fierce degree of loyalty for their humans. They have enchanting, irrepressible personalities.

Although a Mau will always be an outgoing and friendly presence, make no mistake that they will have a special

Chapter 1 – The Egyptian Mau

person on whom they will train their laser-like focus and devotion.

While not necessarily hyperactive, Egyptian Maus keep themselves happily occupied as they go about tending to what they perceive to be their daily "business." Theirs is a doting affection, and one that expects to be at the center of all family activities, even in a household of one.

A Mau can be cleverly mischievous and no cabinet door is safe against his curious paws – for that matter, he's just as likely to open the refrigerator on his own!

Your Mau will cheerfully ride on your shoulder and serve as an unerringly accurate alarm clock. He's anxious to get on with the day and assumes you are – or should be – as well!

Even within the family, however, a Mau would prefer interactions on his own terms, liking to be handled and carried more by some people than by others.

They are highly adaptable as kittens, but once they've settled into their "world," they don't like change. For this reason, relocating older animals including rescues can be challenging and requires a great deal of patience and understanding.

Unique Behaviors

One of the most delightful behaviors exhibited by the Egyptian Mau is referred to as "wiggle tail." This is

Chapter 1 – The Egyptian Mau

reminiscent of the kind of wiggling and tail twitching seen in spraying, but no urine is released when a male or female Mau goes through this dance.

"Wiggle tail" is a uniquely Mau expression of joy and delight, and is in no way a destructive or "naughty" behavior. They will also tread their paws and chortle to indicate a good mood or pleasurable reaction.

Maus also love to designate some household object as "the enemy" and viciously "thwack" the offensive item into submission.

There is absolutely no rhyme or reason to the things your Mau will choose to vilify and then "conquer," but needless to say, the behavior can be pretty amusing to watch so long as spillage and breakage are not involved!

Chapter 1 – The Egyptian Mau

This "thwacking" is in keeping with the breed's great love of toys and games. You don't have to worry about inventing such pastimes for your cat. Your Mau will appear with a toy and proceed to teach you the rules. Your participation and complete attention are required!

You will find many references to the breed's supposed love of playing in water, but this is a highly individualized matter of taste. Almost all Maus will test drinking water with their paws before they begin to sip it.

My Heidi loves to play in the water, so I'm constantly mopping up the area around her bowl. It's the cleanest patch of floor in my house!

With Children and Other Pets

The Mau's personality has often been described as "dog like" due to the breed's tendency to greet its humans at the door and follow them around the house.

For this reason, the Mau gets on well with dogs and with other family pets so long as all the introductions and socialization occurs early in the cat's life.

Once a Mau is set in his ways, it's hard to change his attitude. They are excellent family pets, but will often be quietly anti-social with strangers.

Again, these are not traits that my cat exhibits, but I know other Maus who are less social, and less adaptable to other animals than Heidi.

Chapter 1 – The Egyptian Mau

All cats, regardless of breed, are individuals and should be regarded as such. Take any personality traits for a breed as "guidelines," but allow your cat to be who and what he is by nature.

Maus do fine with children that have been taught to behave appropriately toward animals and will usually just absent themselves if they don't like whatever the kids are doing.

One Cat or Two?

Pairs of Egyptian Mau get along well, especially if they lived together all their lives. Littermates or other young kittens introduced early on are ideal life companions. The breed is highly territorial, however, so later in life pairings don't always go well.

Chapter 1 – The Egyptian Mau

The existing Mau takes the newcomer as an invader and fights can ensue. If your cat has outside privileges don't be surprised if your Mau jumps on the neighbor's dog or cat for daring to set paw in his yard or on his porch.

Again, I strongly discourage allowing cats access to the outdoors in our dangerous modern world unless you have a very secure portion of your yard.

Male or Female

The male or female question, though a standard one, has never really held much weight in my book. The usual argument against adopting male cats is the commonly held belief that all toms spray.

I have owned male cats all my life, kept them exclusively inside, and never had one that sprayed.

This behavior is seen even less often in the Egyptian Mau, although the species does do the "wiggle tail." This is an expression of happiness and is NOT spraying even though it looks much the same.

In my experience, Maus – and in fact all cats – of both genders make excellent pets. People forget that cats, like humans, develop according to their life experiences.

Cats that have been treated well, with kindness and respect, are excellent companions regardless of gender and make very well behaved members of the household.

Chapter 1 – The Egyptian Mau

Frankly, when I am presented with an instance of a cat misbehaving, my tendency is to first look for what the humans are doing wrong rather than blame the "bad" behavior on the animal.

In almost all cases, the cat is simply being a cat and the people with whom he's living don't understand the message he's clearly sending.

Egyptian Mau Clubs and Groups

There are two clubs affiliated with the Cat Fancier's Association that seek to both promote the breed and build a community of breeders and enthusiasts.

The Egyptian Mau Breeders and Fanciers Club was established in 1975 and can be found at www.embc.com, while the The International Egyptian Mau Society is located at www.aime.us. (Note that the latter has multiple language versions for the website content.)

In the United Kingdom, The Egyptian Mau Club at www.egyptianmaus.co.uk is affiliated with The Governing Council of the Cat Fancy.

Another group vital to the welfare of the breed is the Egyptian Mau Rescue Organization (EMRO) at www.emaurescue.org.

This group exists specifically to protect and rehome the Mau breed internationally from Egypt where the cats are

Chapter 1 – The Egyptian Mau

not appreciated for the rare treasure they are in the world of the cat fancy.

Even if you decide that the Egyptian Mau is not the breed for you, the EMRO is doing vital work to protect this ancient breed and, like all animal welfare groups, is in constant need of support.

Among their many programs, EMRO allows interested parties to sponsor individual rescue Maus until they can be placed in loving "forever" homes.

Chapter 1 – The Egyptian Mau

Chapter 2 - Buying an Egyptian Mau Cat

Adopting a pedigreed cat can in no way be compared to simply picking out a kitten from a litter at a friend's house. In instances of unplanned litters, the human "parents" are generally all too ready to place the babies in new homes and get the wandering mother cat "fixed" as soon as possible.

Pedigreed cats are not born by accident and they are not adopted out on a whim. It may come as something of a shock to you to learn that even if you are standing there with checkbook or credit card in hand, you can be turned down by a breeder as a prospective Egyptian Mau owner.

Locating a Breeder

Egyptian Maus are not the kind of cats you find listed in the want ads at the back of the paper. In fact, I would discourage you from even considering any pedigreed cats offered for sale in this fashion as they very likely are coming from backyard kitten mills.

The best venue to locate breeders is a cat show. While you will not be able to actually adopt a cat at the show, you can see the finest examples of the breeder's bloodlines and collect business cards to set up a future appointment.

Later in this book I provide a directory of Egyptian Mau breeders with an online presence. I do want to say, however, that I am categorically not a fan of shipping live animals.

Chapter 2 - Buying an Egyptian Mau Cat

Under optimal circumstances you should find a breeder close to your area. Regardless, however, you should be prepared to go to the cattery in person and accompany your new pet home either by car or plane. If you are flying with a kitten, pay to have the cat in the cabin with you.

No matter what guarantees are made for the safety and security of animals being shipped, the risks are far too great and the stresses too severe. In the vast majority of cases, breeders will not agree to ship kittens anyway, but I do not believe you should even consider this as an option.

While travel costs will add to the expense of acquiring a pedigreed Egyptian Mau, we are talking about the health

Chapter 2 - Buying an Egyptian Mau Cat

and welfare of a living creature both in physical and psychological terms. There is no way to put a price on assuring both are safeguarded to the fullest extent possible.

Conditions of Adoption

You will be asked by the breeder to agree to some specific conditions in writing or you will certainly be denied the right to adopt an Egyptian Mau from the cattery in question.

Mandatory Spaying and Neutering

One of the most important provisions of the adoption agreement is your assent to having the cat spayed or neutered before it reaches six months of age.

In the vast majority of cases, you will be adopting an Egyptian Mau that has been designated as "pet quality," meaning there are perceived flaws that deviate from the show standard for the breed.

While these "mistakes" may render the animal unsuitable for being shown in exhibition, you likely won't be able to see the problem even when it's pointed out to you.

The point of the spaying and the neutering, in part, however, is to protect the integrity of the breed's genetics and to prevent undesirable traits from being passed on.

Breeders also do not want to contribute to the terrible epidemic of unwanted companion animals that leads to so many pets being abandoned annually and euthanized when no homes can be found for them.

Future Surrenders

For this reason, you will also be asked to agree that if you cannot keep the Mau for any reason, you will never sell it to another person or worse yet give it to an animal shelter. If you must surrender the cat, you should contact the breeder.

All breeders will take cats back rather than see them abandoned or placed in shelters only to be needlessly euthanized.

The breeder's focus is rightfully on the welfare of the cat, and that extends to matters of re-homing should that become necessary.

Initial Health Evaluation

It's standard protocol to require a newly adopted pedigreed cat to be evaluated by a veterinarian within 72 hours of leaving the cattery. You will be asked to provide written proof of this fact.

The initial health evaluation is intended to provide a baseline for the health guarantee that is part of every adoption agreement. The vet visit confirms that when you received the kitten, the baby was in good health.

Lifestyle Inquiries

Although these questions are typically not asked in written format, the breeder will want to know about your home and your lifestyle. This isn't intended to be a matter of giving you the "third degree," so please don't be offended.

Remember that breeders are passionately committed to the welfare of their cats; they want to know that they're going to good homes.

Especially with a breed as interactive as the Egyptian Mau, the breeder will want to ascertain if have the time to give your new pet the attention and companionship it will crave.

In the weeks after the adoption, don't be surprised if the breeder calls you up to see how things are going. This isn't just checking up on the cat, but also to give you an opportunity to ask questions.

The owners of pedigreed cats should always be on friendly terms with the breeder from whom the animal was acquired. Your breeder is an expert on the Egyptian Mau an invaluable source of advice and information for you as you begin your life with your new pet.

Your Questions for the Breeder

Even though the breeder will want to get a lot of information from you, information should flow freely. You

Chapter 2 - Buying an Egyptian Mau Cat

want to be dealing with someone who will freely answer your questions.

Generally this is not a problem. People who run catteries like nothing quite as much as talking about their cats!

Some of the questions you should ask include the following items, but don't limit yourself. The whole idea of this exchange is to ensure that both sides feel good about the adoption and about the living creature whose welfare and happiness should be central to the whole process.

- Are the kitten's parents healthy?
- What are their personalities like?
- Do they both live at the cattery?
- If not, where does the other parent reside?
- Can you see the health records for both parents?
- Can you meet and interact with the parents?
- Has the kitten received any vaccinations?
- Will those records be passed to you?
- Have other medical treatments been required?
- Has the kitten been dewormed?
- What health guarantees are included?
- Are references available?

In the matter of references, make sure you see not only written recommendations, but are also provided with the names and contact information of people willing to speak with you.

Chapter 2 - Buying an Egyptian Mau Cat

The Importance of Socialization

Typically kittens remain in catteries until they are about three months old. By that time they have been fully weaned and are reliably using both a litter box and a scratching post.

During the time the baby lives at the cattery, it should be exposed to various situations that help to achieve good socialization. As young cats, Egyptian Maus are highly adaptable, but as they age, they become used to their circumstances and less open to change.

Good socialization will help the kitten to have an easy transition to your home and to be better adjusted as an adult. Most Maus will be somewhat shy around strangers, but you don't want your pet to be fearful of people who come into your home on a regular basis.

Organized socialization programs should include all of the following elements.

- *Daily handling.* Egyptian Maus are gregarious by nature and like to be a part of whatever is going on around them. They respond happily to being handled as kittens, although as adults they often prefer to initiate the interaction. This varies by individual.

- *Free exploration time.* This is also simply a matter of catering to the Mau's normally high level of curiosity. I wouldn't necessarily call the breed nosey but your cat will know every nook and cranny of your home, and few doors will be safe against those clever and dexterous paws.

- *Interaction with other cats.* Again, Maus are very social as kittens, so they should have lots of time to interact with other cats. If you're introducing a Mau to a household with other pets, this is the ideal time to do it. As adults, Maus can be territorial and occasionally a little jealous of their "special" people.

- *Access to plentiful toys.* Egyptian Maus are very playful. They love toys and are especially fond of long games of fetch. Find out what kind of toys the babies have liked at the cattery and get the same items for your home.

- *Exposure to normal household sounds.* Typically Egyptian Maus are not nervous, but it is a good idea for them to be familiar with normal household sounds including appliances at a young age. All Maus are prone to "thwacking" objects around the house, but this more an expression of playful dominance than fear.

Even for a gregarious breed like the Egyptian Mau, adoption still represents leaving the only environment they have known for a new home. Good socialization makes that change much easier.

Chapter 2 - Buying an Egyptian Mau Cat

Judging a Kitten's Health

Even though you have come to the cattery for the express purpose of adopting a kitten, always ask for permission to handle the cat. You may be asked to use hand sanitizer first. Don't be offended. This is for the protection of the kitten.

Beyond the fact that playing with an adorable baby kitten is a wonderful experience, it's also a great chance to evaluate the baby's muscle tone as well as the quality and texture of its coat.

Mau babies should have soft, clean coats that are completely intact with no thin spots. Check at the base of the tail, under the "arms" and behind the ears for any black gravel-like residue. This is known as "flea dirt" and is actually excreted bits of blood the parasites leave behind.

A kitten with one or two fleas is not being neglected or kept in poor conditions. The war on fleas is constant for all catteries, especially in warm weather. It's almost impossible not to bring the persistent pests in the house on your shoes or pants legs.

If fleas are present, you want to make sure the problem is taken care of before the kitten comes into your home, especially if other animals are present.

During all of this handling, the kitten should be watching you with a bright, curious gaze. There should be no crusty discharge or running of either the eyes or the nose. Also listen for any sneezing or snuffling that could indicate an upper respiratory infection.

Chapter 2 - Buying an Egyptian Mau Cat

Interact with the kitten using toys. You're looking for a happy, pouncing reaction that indicates active interest and good health. No kitten of less than 9 months of age will react to catnip, however, and some cats never develop an interest in the herb.

Adoption Paperwork

A great deal of paperwork is involved in adopting a pedigreed cat. The forms will vary by cattery, but typically a written adoption agreement will include the following:

- A description of the breed being adopted including color and pattern.
- The gender of the kitten being adopted.
- The names of the kitten's parents.
- The agreed upon price.
- Complete contact information for both the buyer and seller.

You will agree to provide the cat with regular veterinary care and appropriate grooming. If, for any reason, you have to return the cat to the breeder, you must have the animal tested within the same week for fecal parasites, ringworm, and FELV/FIV.

The kitten is not to be sold or given away without the written permission of the breeder.

Chapter 2 - Buying an Egyptian Mau Cat

Declawing Expressly Forbidden

All adoption agreements expressly forbid that the cat be declawed. The practice is illegal in Europe and also in many parts of the United States, and for good reason.

The surgery requires the amputation of the last joint of each of the cat's toes. The procedure is painful, affects the animal's mobility, deprives the cats of its best means of self-defense – and is completely unnecessary!

The answer to problem scratching is not radical mutilation, but proper training, regular claw clipping, and free access to scratching posts and trees.

Genetic Health Conditions

All adoption agreements include a health guarantee and details about any evaluations the animal has received. This includes known genetic conditions associated with the breed.

(Please refer to the chapter on health for more details on this topic.)

In relation to the adoption agreement, however, understand that details of health evaluations should not be couched as total guarantees that no genetic problems are present in the cattery's bloodline. Many of these conditions cannot be detected early in life, nor conclusively prevented.

The only information that can be provided is records of tests conducted, and an indication that problems have not surfaced in the kitten's parents. That fact alone typically indicates the offspring will be free from genetic problems, but there are no absolute assurances that can or should be made.

Bringing Your Egyptian Mau Home

Egyptian Mau kittens tend to handle the transition from the cattery to their new homes with aplomb. It is still advisable, however, to make as few changes as possible in the kitten's daily routine, especially in regard to litter and food.

Cats are particular about texture, which applies to both their diet and their litter. Some cats love chunky food and others will touch nothing but pate. One cat is perfectly happy with gravel, while another won't use anything but fine sand.

Chapter 2 - Buying an Egyptian Mau Cat

Since you don't want your cat going "off" its food or litter box, get this information from the breeder and acquire the same products including bowl and litter box types.

Introduce changes slowly, with the understanding that often these preferences are set for life even when a cat is very young.

Make sure that all the toys you get for your baby Mau are kitten safe and do not present a choking hazard. Items with strings, feathers, bells, or other attachments should be "with supervision only."

Because the Mau's coat is short and tight, these cats require very little grooming beyond nail clipping. Still, it's best to have all the implements you need on hand and to get your cat used to its grooming routine from kittenhood forward.

The Business of Kitten Proofing

All kittens are insatiably curious and have a conflated view of their own abilities, but Mau babies take those qualities to the extreme. Don't underestimate your new pet's ability to get into trouble fast!

Take a good look at the area(s) where the kitten will be spending most of its time. Remove anything in which the baby can become tangled.

Pay special attention to electrical cords, which also present "topple over" dangers and the risk of electrocution from

Chapter 2 - Buying an Egyptian Mau Cat

chewing. Use tape to secure the wires to the baseboards and cap all electrical outlets.

Install baby latches on all cabinet doors, especially those where household chemicals and other dangerous substances are kept. Also remove all houseplants.

So many houseplants are toxic to cats that I have personally instigated a "no plants" policy. Any form of lily is especially dangerous, but almost all plants will, at the least, cause gastrointestinal distress. If you do want to keep plants, I advise having them in a room to which your cat does not have access.

Chapter 2 - Buying an Egyptian Mau Cat

The First Few Days

Even if no other pets are present in the home, it's generally best to keep the kitten confined to one small room, even a bathroom, for the first few days.

If there are other pets in the house, the bathroom door forms the perfect "demilitarized zone." Cats live in a world completely dominated by scents, so safe sniffing and a little paw play under a closed door will ease a lot of the initial angst of a face-to-face meeting.

When pets are directly introduced for the first time, let the animals work it out. You should be a calm observer. Don't let your pets pick up on any tension emanating from you. If a rescue is necessary, you'll be right there.

Kittens are typically fully established in a household in about a week, and any territorial issues with other pets are also generally resolved within that same period.

Approximate Costs

A pet quality Egyptian Mau costs from $585-$750 / £350-£450. Show quality females are $1000+ / £600+ while males are often sold for more than $1675+ / £1000+.

Prices can vary widely by breeder, location, age, and bloodline. Remember to factor in the cost of travel, including airfare and hotel accommodations. Again, I strongly discourage the shipping of live animals. The chances for life-long trauma or potential tragedy are simply too great.

Chapter 2 - Buying an Egyptian Mau Cat

Chapter 2 - Buying an Egyptian Mau Cat

Chapter 3 – Daily Care Needs

Many people are under the mistaken impression that cats are aloof loners. While some breeds do like more time by themselves, or choose to elegantly position themselves across the room on the sofa rather than be in the thick of things, the Egyptian Mau is not one of them!

Maus are more likely to be riding around on your shoulder or trotting happily at your heels to see what's next on the day's agenda. These cats require interaction with their humans. They have emotional as well as physical needs.

Because they are highly intelligent and will quickly learn your routine, Egyptian Maus don't suffer unduly from separation anxiety. They will, however, be waiting at the door at the appointed hour when they expect you to be home from work.

If you're late, a Mau will likely demand an explanation, at which time you'll be thankful he posses a more melodious voice and patient nature than a Siamese under the same circumstances.

Feline Communication 101

Anyone who has ever lived with a cat knows that they are not animals that will tolerate being ignored or that suffer boredom well.

An Egyptian Mau will get his opinion across, pleasantly, but insistently – no matter how long it takes his human to clue into what he's saying.

The higher your level of interaction with your pet, the more you will come to know your Mau as a "person," with uniquely individual quirks and expressive tendencies.

Knowing your cat's behavior and daily attitude intimately is one of the best safeguards you can afford your pet. If you think something is wrong physically, or behaviorally, go with your gut.

Let me give you a case in point. I once lived with an incredibly intelligent Russian Blue, also a very devoted and interactive breed.

Chapter 3 – Daily Care Needs

After showing no interest whatsoever in the space behind the refrigerator, my pet suddenly became obsessed. I fussed. He insisted. I ignored him.

Then the water started seeping up between the boards of the hardwood floor! My cat had been trying to tell me for almost a week that there was a pinhole leak in the water line to the refrigerator icemaker.

Had I listened to him, I would have been spared considerable expense, a fact I think he pointed out to me with an inimitable feline expression of, "I tried to tell you."

Understand from the beginning that when you bring an Egyptian Mau, or really any cat, into your life, you are establishing a relationship with a highly intelligent creature.

He may be another species, but he's still part of your life. He regards you as "his," and he will try to communicate with you.

Since a cat does not have the physical capacity to speak our language, the burden of learning a new vocabulary rests solidly with us.

This means crossing not just a language, but also a species barrier, and realizing that your cat's sensory perception of the world is entirely different than your own.

Everyone knows, for instance, that cats are very good at ignoring their humans when they're getting scolded in a raised tone of voice. This isn't, however, a sign of obstinacy or arrogance. A cat's hearing is designed to detect high-pitched, subtle sounds.

Whisper to your cat and see what happens. His ears will immediately become alert, rotating in place to zero in on the sound of your voice. You will instantly have your pet's attention.

There is also a misconception that cats don't like men, which isn't at all true. Cats simply hear women's voices more clearly. If you're a man with a low, deep voice you may just sound like a rumbled blur to a cat.

Cats will actually respond more readily to hand gestures and visual cues than spoken words. Often a cat that is completely recalcitrant to "orders" will be much more likely to follow unspoken commands reliably.

Managing Your Cat's Diet

Yet another of the many myths constantly perpetuated about cats is that they are finicky eaters. It would be more accurate to say that they are particular, and since we humans do the same thing, we shouldn't be casting aspersions on the cat's tastes. I, myself, wouldn't choke down a Brussels sprout on a dare.

Cats have very definite individual likes and dislikes that extend not just to flavor, but also to food texture and even the type of bowl used.

Chapter 3 – Daily Care Needs

Emphasize Quality Foods

Cats are carnivores. Their diets should be primarily protein based. It is not a good idea to simply leave a bowl of dry food out at all times.

For one thing, with an Egyptian Mau, that won't get you anything but an overweight cat! For as sleek and graceful as the breed is by nature, they are also chow hands and will quite readily pack on the pounds if you're not vigilant with their portions.

In managing your cat's diet, strive for a good balance of high-quality wet and dry food served in measured amounts.

Wet Food is Important

The number one reason cited for feeding a cat dry food exclusively is less mess in the litter box. There is no validity to this assumption. Excessive amounts of waste and extreme litter box odor indicate that you're feeding your cat something he isn't digesting well.

This is not, an indication that all wet food should be eliminated, but rather that a different product be chosen. Cats should always receive canned food, which is an important source of both protein and dietary moisture.

Chapter 3 – Daily Care Needs

Visually Check Body Weight

You don't really need a scale to decide if your cat is gaining too much weight. While your cat is standing, look down at his body shape. There should be a slight indentation behind the rib cage and above the hips.

That area is your cat's "waist." If you can't see it, then you likely know from personal experience it's time for kitty to go on a diet!

Obesity can lead to a myriad of health conditions in cats (and humans) including diabetes, high blood pressure, and arthritic joints. Don't overfeed either dry or wet food, and don't let your cat get started on human food.

Egyptian Maus are notoriously diet resistant. Once they get a taste for a particular item, especially some forbidden treat; they may well go off their regular food entirely until they get what they want.

Not only are they skilled little beggars, they are also incredibly stubborn. If you give in to a Mau once and let him have his way, it's pretty much "game over!"

In such instances, you haven't just lost a single battle; you've surrendered the entire dietary war -- much to your cat's satisfaction, but also to his physical detriment. Don't give in!

Chapter 3 – Daily Care Needs

Dangerous Toxic Foods

Many human food items are highly toxic to cats including, but not limited to:
- alcoholic beverages
- avocados
- grapes and raisins
- eggs
- garlic
- onions and chives
- all types of yeast dough
- caffeine in any form
- chocolate

The cacao seeds in chocolate contain methylxanthines, which are also found in many beverages including soda.

The range of symptoms resulting from exposure to these items are serious and potentially life threatening:

- excessive thirst
- panting
- vomiting
- diarrhea
- irregular heartbeat
- seizures
- tremors

Also make certain that your cat has no access to foods containing the sweetener xylitol, which can cause liver failure.

Chapter 3 – Daily Care Needs

Do not give your cat any salty treats, which create a risk of dehydration. Cats should never go extended periods of time without water or eat anything that causes excessive thirst.

The Truth about Cats and Milk

Just because cats like milk doesn't mean they should have milk or even that milk is good for them. Every mammal produces milk that is appropriate for its own young. Does it stand to reason that a cat would benefit from consuming cow's milk?

Of course your cat will take milk, or for that mater ice cream, but the truth is that cats don't make enough of the enzyme lactase to digest milk. In most cases, too much milk will give cats a case of severe gastrointestinal upset and diarrhea.

In other words, your cat can be just as lactose intolerant as a human! If you or someone you know has this problem, then you understand just how uncomfortable the condition can be. Why would you want to put your pet through this?

Adult cats do not need milk and they don't derive any nutritional benefit from consuming it. Occasional dishes of milk or cream as a treat are fine, but discontinue the practice immediately if your cat exhibits any signs of having an upset stomach. Not only will your pet be extremely uncomfortable, you'll have to clean his box!

Chapter 3 – Daily Care Needs

Free Feeding

With some breeds you absolutely cannot leave food in the bowl at all times, a practice called "free feeding," and the Mau is one of those breeds.

Maus love their groceries! If you let your cat get away with it, he'll always be on the prowl for his next snack. Once you allow this kind of behavior to get started, don't think it will be easy to put your cat on a diet.

Maus are perfectly capable of engaging in protracted hunger strikes until they get the food they want, in the amount they want.

In this contest of wills, the Mau pretty much always wins, so regulate the availability of food from the moment your willful little Egyptian beauty enters the house.

Selecting Appropriate Foods

Make sure that the first ingredient on any food label is meat. As carnivores, cats cannot and should not be made vegetarians, either on purpose or by accident.

You can take it as a standard that the less you pay for canned or dry cat food the more likely the item is to be packed with grain fillers. These ingredients provide no nutritional benefit for your cat whatsoever.

Consult with your breeder to find out what brands your Egyptian Mau is accustomed to eating, and what foods would be used had the kitten matured in their care. You can, as a point of comparison, ask your veterinarian for the same advice.

Typically the two restraints on dietary selection are product availability and budget. Ordering pet food online has largely eradicated the issue of availability, but we all have to watch our finances.

My best advice to you is to buy the highest quality wet or dry food that you can afford. Make sure the primary ingredient is meat.

Don't let your cat free feed, and never allow your pet to get hooked on "people food." Pair these strategies with a constant supply of clean, fresh drinking water, and you will be covering the nutritional bases for your Egyptian Mau.

The Importance of Hydration

In keeping with their fastidious nature, cats won't drink from dirty water dishes, and they don't like water that has become stale.

Not all Egyptian Maus will play in their water bowls the way mine does, but most will test a few drops on their paw before drinking.

Like many breeds, these cats may be better about drinking adequate amounts of water if they are given a running supply via a recirculating water fountain. Such units retail for $30/£23 and many cats thoroughly enjoy using them.

Chapter 3 – Daily Care Needs

Approximating Food Costs

There are too many options in the area of cat food at too many price points to arrive at any accurate estimation of feeding costs. I can only offer a conservative estimate based on my own experiences.

Typically, I spend about $50/£33 each month on each cat for wet food, and around $25/£17 on dry.

Feeding Schedule

On a daily basis, offer your cats around .25-.50 cups of dry food (60-120 grams) and 5.5 ounces / 14.17 grams of wet food.

Buying Food Bowls

Although Egyptian Maus are not as a breed prone to suffering from "whisker stress," this condition can occur with any kind of cat.

The animal experiences an unpleasant rubbing sensation as the whiskers come in contact with sides of a normally shaped bowl.

If your cat picks up bites of food and quickly drops them on to the floor before eating them, whisker stress is likely the culprit behind the behavior.

Chapter 3 – Daily Care Needs

The solution is to use a slightly elevated dish that looks like a shallow tray. Normal food and water bowls cost about $5-$10 / £3-£7, while a whisker stress tray retails for $25/£16.

Litter Box "Business"

For many people who do not want to have to walk a dog, the fact that cats can live cleanly inside using a litter box is a huge plus of having a companion feline.

Litter box maintenance is not, however, something you can neglect. It's a daily chore, not weekly. Cats are very clean, and they are highly sensitive to odors. They won't use a filthy box, and may well do their business someplace inappropriate instead.

When I hear of a cat being given up for poor litter box habits, my reaction is generally very negative and completely aimed at the humans in the equation.

In my experience, there are two main reasons why cats go "off" their boxes: illness and bad housekeeping on the part of their human!

Again, try to think with feline logic. When a cat gets into the litter box to "go" and experiences pain from an undiagnosed urinary tract or bladder infection, they assume the pain and the location are linked.

The poor creature then goes in search of some place to do its business pain free!

Chapter 3 – Daily Care Needs

As for good litter box maintenance on your part, consider this. A cat has 200 million odor receptors to your 5 million. What smells bad to you *reeks* to a cat!

When a cat goes off his box, first get him evaluated by a vet, and then evaluate your own performance in the housekeeping department. After that, consider the type of litter and design of the box you're using.

Some cats just don't like going in an open litter box where they can be observed. The issue could also be the type of litter offered. Your cat may prefer sand rather than gravel, for instance.

Never introduce sudden changes in regard to the type of box and texture of litter. Cats get used to using one thing and typically do not adjust well unless any difference is introduced slowly.

If you do want to switch to a different litter, begin by mixing a little of the new material in with the old, gradually increasing the amount over a period of weeks.

For box types, set up the new pan adjacent to the old one filled with the same type of litter. Never take away the old box until the cat has fully accepted the new one.

If your cat has gone outside of the box, that spot is now marked in the cat's mind. In order to eradicate the scents he can detect and you can't, use an enzymatic cleaner like the products made by Nature's Miracle. Depending on the size of the container, the items are priced at $5-$10/£3-£6.

Considering Available Litters

The traditional choice for a cat's litter is gravel or clay. This style is very cheap. You can buy 10 lbs. (4.53 kg) for just $2.50-$5.00 (£2-£4). The problem, however, is that clay is not particularly good at absorbing moisture and controlling odor.

Clumping Litters

In recent years fine sand that clumps when wet has become very popular. This type of litter is available in many formulations like those designed for multiple cats.

Mainstream clumping litters are priced in bulk with 42 lbs. (19 kg) selling for about $18 / £12. The "designer" variations for multiple cats or superior odor control are more expensive, selling for around $30 / £20 for 1.4 lbs. (.63 kg).

I use clumping litters with my cats, but I don't like how easily the sand scatters. There are, however, effective ways to deal with this problem.

Litter Trapping Mats

If you do decide to use clumping sand litter, consider getting a mat to put under the box to trap the scattered material.

The mats come in a variety of sizes and retail for around $20 / £12. They are made of coarse material that catches and holds the litter. To clean the mat, just take it outside and shake out the debris.

Chapter 3 – Daily Care Needs

No Flushing!

The most important thing to remember about any clumping litter is not to flush the material unless the box specifically says it's all right to do so.

I had a friend who tried this. For all practical purposes, the litter turned to concrete in his pipes. He had to have the whole bathroom ripped out and new pipes put in. The "rotor rooter" tool couldn't budge the clog!

Green Litters

In keeping with the growing environmental consciousness we are seeing in our society, cat owners now have options for environmentally friendly litters made from plant-based materials.

One of the most popular and inexpensive of this genre is shaved pine like that used in hamster habitats. Most cats not only dislike the feel of the material, but it is so lightweight they literally fling it around the house.

I'll be honest that I've never had any luck with either pine or ground corncob litters. Perhaps if a kitten was raised to use these materials from the point of being litter box trained initially these substances will work, but in general I give these litters a thumbs down.

As a point of price comparison, 20 lbs. (9.07 kg) of pine shavings sell for approximately $10 / £7.

Silica Gel Crystals

Silica gel absorbent crystals are a new and interesting innovation in litter box products. The biodegradable amorphous silica traps the urine and inhibits bacterial growth.

I have not tried crystal litters with my cats, but the material looks and feels very much like gravel, which leads me to believe picky litter box users might be more receptive to it.

The crystals are lighter than clay, but the issue with cats really is the texture. You can purchase 8 lbs. / 3.62 kg of crystals for approximately $16 / £11.

Picking a Litter Box

There are all sizes and shapes of litter box available on the market but all are a variation of the traditional open pan, a covered box, or a mechanized self-scooping unit.

Obviously the "standard" open pan is the easiest to find and the cheapest at around $6-$10 / £4-£6. Certainly a pan of this sort works, but it has definite drawbacks:

- excessive scattering
- high odor
- excessive dampness
- unsightly appearance

With a combination of a litter trapping mat, a screen, and air fresheners, these can all be managed. We've already

Chapter 3 – Daily Care Needs

discussed mats, which retail for about $20 / £12. A folding screen to hide the box is about $10 / £6, and air fresheners are $5 / £3 each.

So, in the end, your $6 / £4 litter box may cost you $40/£24 with the recurring expense of trading out the air fresheners. The bottom line is that you may think you're getting off cheap with a traditional pan, but they're higher maintenance all the way around.

I prefer covered boxes, as do my cats. The lids make the mess much less unsightly and are outfitted with carbon filters to help cut down on the dust from my preferred sand litter. Depending on the size you select, you'll pay $30-$50 / £20-£33 for a good, sturdy, covered litter box.

I will admit that I did buy an automatic self-scooping litter box when they first came out, only to play witness to varied reactions on the part of my cats.

One fled in terror from the "monster," a second spent the whole afternoon getting in and out of the box to watch the rake go across the litter, and a third did his best to dismantle the "thing" and figure out how it worked.

The concept is great. The cat does his business. On the way out of the box, he triggers a motion sensor. A rake descends into the box, scooping the soiled litter into a receptacle that closes automatically.

When it's full, you snap the lid in place and throw the whole thing away. On a whole, you use less litter, but you do have to pay for the disposable plastic receptacles.

I loved the mechanical box, but in a multi-cat household, the reactions were too mixed. I have seen other variations on this idea, but I haven't spent any money on trying them out. The experiments are just too rich for my blood at $150 to $200 / £90 to £120 per unit.

The Playful and Interactive Egyptian Mau

There are many cat breeds that are not receptive to training, but not the Egyptian Mau. These smart and interactive little souls are up for just about anything. If you can't come up with a new trick, they'll invent the routine and teach you!

Chapter 3 – Daily Care Needs

Maus are sometimes referred to as being "dog like" because unlike many cats, they do seem to have an innate desire to please their humans.

Although many are standoffish with total strangers, mine have always welcomed regular guests with enthusiasm – sometimes dropping toys at the feet of the newcomer with an inquisitive chirp as if to say, "Do you know this game?"

My best advice about training a Mau is to cater to the animal's obvious interests and to work to extrapolate on the behavior.

As I described in the forward, I held up a sewing hoop by accident one day only to see Heidi bound right through it. Now she'll vault through a tunnel on cue with magnificent grace.

This is one of the things I absolutely love about sharing my life with an Egyptian Mau. They're smart, responsive, and fun!

I really don't think there's any end to the series of complex behavior these cats can muster. The happier they are making you, their beloved human, the more they will perform.

Remember, however, that Maus do have a tendency to pack on the pounds, so rather than direct behavior with treats as rewards use fulsome verbal praise instead. I've never had any breed of cat that enjoys being talked to quite as much as the Egyptian Mau.

Chapter 3 – Daily Care Needs

Typically I tell cat owners to keep any training sessions under 15 minutes so the cat doesn't get bored, but this really isn't an issue with a Mau. They'll keep going until you drop!

From riding on my shoulder to giving me a high five when I put out my hand, Heidi has unerringly learned every behavior I've suggested and come up with more than a few on her own.

Scientists believe that cats are capable of learning 35-50 words, but as the doting parent of an Egyptian Mau, I'm convinced she understands every word I say. I believe that the more you talk and interact with any cat breed, the more responsive they will become.

Scratching

Chapter 3 – Daily Care Needs

I've found the Egyptian Mau to be a very well behaved breed with their claws, but do make sure your pet has a good scratching post.

A standard carpet covered pole retailing for around $30/£20 will suffice for simple claw sharpening, but if you really want to make your cat blissfully happy, pop for an elaborate cat tree.

Sure, you'll be forking out anywhere from $100 (£65) to $300 (£197), but your Mau will have so much fun, and you'll be so entertained by his antics, it'll be worth the price.

Heidi is not a destructive scratcher, but if you do have a cat bent on destroying the furniture, I recommend either herbal anti-scratching products or double-sided adhesive strips.

Both pennyroyal and orange essence sprays are highly effective and inexpensive, retailing for $12-$15 / £7.87-£9.84. Double-sided adhesive strips sell for $8-$10 / £5.25-$6.56 per package.

Minimalist Mau Grooming

With their sleek, tight coats, Egyptian Maus are very easy to groom, requiring little more than a light brushing once a week. This not only keeps any stray hair down, but it's good for your pet's skin.

Chapter 3 – Daily Care Needs

I like pincushion brushes, which have widely spaced individual bristles on a bed of rubber. They sell for about $7-$10.

Chapter 4 – Health Care Facts

The Egyptian Mau is an extremely healthy and robust breed – almost unusually so. There are no known genetic issues with Maus. They are even remarkably free of cardiomyopathy, a deadly condition that can surface in virtually any type of cat.

Attention to Routine Health Care

Your veterinarian is your partner in building the solid foundation of your cat's primary health care program. While any small animal veterinarian is qualified to work with your cat, I personally prefer to take my animals to a feline-specific clinic for a number of reasons.

- Feline-only vets stay on the cutting edge of medical development in the treatment of conditions exclusive to cats.

- The offices are much quieter. With no barking dogs or other unusual animals to startle your pets, the cats stay calmer and suffer less from anxiety. There are also fewer strange odors that put cats on high alert.

- Feline-only clinics understand "cat people" and our devotion to our animals. No one thinks anything about you admitting that you're a self-proclaimed "crazy cat lady," and you will never hear the abhorrent phrase, "just a cat."

Chapter 4 – Health Care Facts

If you are interviewing a new vet, make an appointment to go in without your cat. Explain that you are coming to meet the doctor and to see the clinic and that you are perfectly happy to pay for a regular office visit.

Remember that veterinarians are medical professionals with a full roster of patients. Prepare your questions in advance and don't overstay. If you like what you see and hear, schedule a second visit that will include your cat.

The second visit is still for purposes of evaluation. You want to see how the vet and the techs interact with your pet.

- Is your cat reasonably relaxed in the office setting?

- Are you comfortable with how your cat is handled and treated?

Make sure that you are satisfied with the doctor, the staff, and the clinic before moving on to what will likely be your Mau's first official procedure, spaying or neutering.

Spaying and Neutering

The reason you are required to spay or neuter pet quality pedigreed cats is not only to help curb the population explosion of unwanted companion animals, but also to protect the genetic quality of the breed.

Chapter 4 – Health Care Facts

Reputable catteries work hard to constantly cultivate and improve their bloodlines. They do not want to see genetic flaws, no matter how minor, passed on, nor do they want to see mixed breed cats produced from their animals.

Either procedure should be performed within the first six months of the cat's life. There are inexpensive options for the surgeries, running as low as $50 (£32.82), but I would counsel against being driven by price considerations alone on this matter.

Unless you've had cats before and are working with a vet with whom you have a long-standing relationship, the spaying or neutering procedure is likely the first major medical event you will experience with your new pet.

If at all possible, it's to your advantage to have the surgery performed by the vet who will treat your cat for the rest of its life. All of the medical records will be in one place, and the vet will have an understanding of your cat's personality and specific reactions to the clinic environment.

Let me give you an example. I had a Domestic Shorthair who tolerated anesthesia extremely well, but he was so lazy and sleepy by nature, it took him forever to wake up after one of his dental cleanings.

My vet knew that one of the techs needed to hold the cat and basically annoy him into waking up so I could take him home. Left to his own devices, he'd happily have slept until the next day!

Chapter 4 – Health Care Facts

Recommended Vaccinations

For most people, the idea that companion animals are routinely vaccinated against infectious diseases is a given. The topic has been controversial, however, for reasons similar to concerns expressed about vaccinations for children and links to conditions like autism.

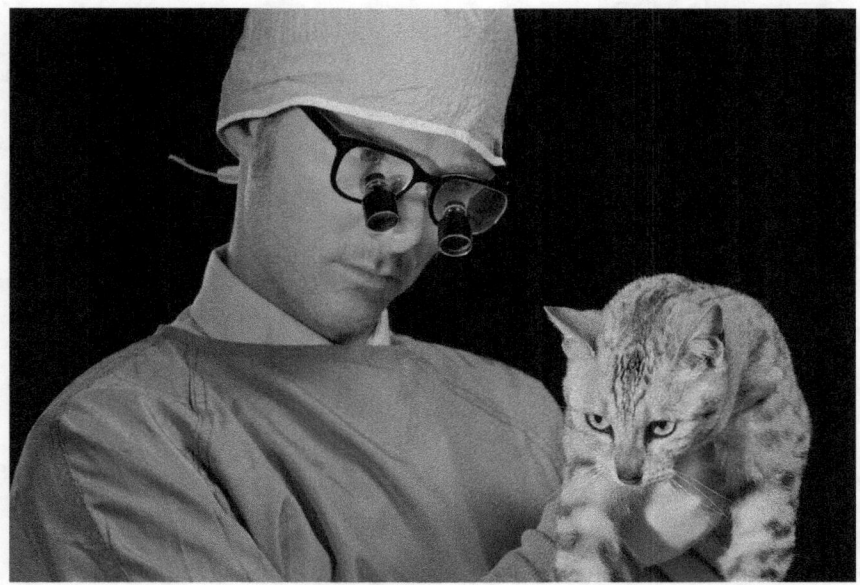

In companion animals, the primary worry is over tumors that can develop at the site of the injection. Some vaccinations, like rabies, are required by law, but others may be administered at the discretion of the owner and veterinarian based on the cat's access to the outdoors and its exposure to other cats.

This is a matter that should be decided in consultation with your vet and after you have conducted further research on

Chapter 4 – Health Care Facts

your own. I have followed both paths, and have experienced no problems with my animals.

I believe that all cats, regardless of breed, are strictly indoor pets, which decreases the risk that my animals will be exposed to infectious disease. In some instances, the decision was based on other factors relevant to the cat's overall wellbeing.

A Somali that I inherited hated going to the vet clinic with a passion. She finally threw a fit so severe that she had a heart attack and flat lined. The vet quickly revived her and suggested that unless it was an emergency, the cat stay at home from that day forward!

I followed the advice, and the cat lived into a healthy old age, ultimately dying of a stroke. In the intervening years, she required only one medical procedure, a tooth extraction. I gave her a mild sedative prescribed by the vet before we left the house and all was well.

Obviously this is another instance in which all concerned benefited from my close working relationship with an exceptional veterinarian.

If you have doubts about vaccinations, the recommended shots that you will want to discuss with your vet include the following:

Distemper Combo

- Typically administered at 6 weeks of age.

Chapter 4 – Health Care Facts

- Boosters every 3-4 weeks until 16 weeks of age.
- A booster at one year.
- Subsequent boosters every 3 years for life.
- Protects against: panleukopenia (FPV or feline infectious enteritis), rhinotracheitis (FVR, an upper respiratory / pulmonary infection), calicivirus (causes respiratory infections)
- May include protection against Chlamydophilia, which causes conjunctivitis.
- Cost varies.

Feline Leukemia

- Give at 2 months.
- Booster 3-4 weeks later.
- Annual boosters for life.
- Cost varies.

Rabies

- Typically mandated by local law.
- Proof of annual compliance required.
- Cost approximately $40 (£26) per injection.

Understanding Feline Preventative Healthcare

One of the reasons that the famous "dog whisperer" Cesar Millan is so effective in dealing with dogs – and moreover, with their humans – is that he encourages the people to try to see the world through their pet's eyes.

Feline behavioral expert Jackson Galaxy does something similar in his program, "My Cat from Hell" for Animal

Planet. I've always found the name of that program amusing, because the perception seems to be that dealing with cats is so much harder than dealing with dogs.

When I was in college, I found it almost impossible to learn any of the Romance language like French or Spanish, but I was able to do reasonably well in German, which seemed more straightforward.

I think this is a good analogy to bring to the table in trying to understand your cat. I cannot stress strongly enough that every cat is a "person" in his own right, but there are some ways they see and interact with the world that are crucial for their humans to understand.

In terms of health care, nothing is more important than viewing how your cat regards pain. Far too many times I've heard cat owners say, "I had no idea he was sick, and when I finally realized something was wrong, it was too late."

Follow up questions then reveal that the cat had spent days or even weeks protectively isolating itself in some quiet spot. Cats are not necessarily stoic creatures; they feel pain. They don't just go off somewhere and "rest up" to magically get over their illnesses. Cats are survivors.

As predators, they see the world in terms of prey and "not prey." If a cat is in pain, and not feeling well, he is vulnerable. He is in danger of becoming prey to a larger, healthier predator. He isolates himself as protection, and he does everything he possibly can do to hide his pain.

Chapter 4 – Health Care Facts

You will know your cat better than anyone. If you have a loving, attentive Egyptian Mau that suddenly is not greeting you at the door every night, or who has lost interest in his beloved game of paper wad fetch? Something is wrong!

It's amazing to me how many people don't want to be perceived as over-protective, running to the vet just because they think something is wrong.

It's your job to be over protective! If you think something is wrong, it probably is! Go with your gut, and have your cat checked out. Many feline health conditions can deteriorate rapidly if left untreated. Don't take that risk!

On a daily basis, as you handle your cat, be aware of any changes in muscle tone or body shape and sensitivity. Your Mau will just think he's getting a great petting session, but this is a perfect opportunity for you to be aware of anything that literally does not feel right to you.

Watch for other signs including, but not limited to:

- Changes in the cat's weight. A healthy cat will have a good pad of fat over the ribs, but you should still be able to feel the bones just slightly underneath that soft layer.

- Differences in how the cat walks, runs, and jumps. Changes in movement suggest problems with potential joint pain, damage to a muscle, or even the presence of a growth.

Chapter 4 – Health Care Facts

- A runny nose or one that is dry and cracked. A healthy cat will have a clean, moist nose with no sign of discharge, clear or discolored.

- Running or "mattering" of the eyes. Your cat's eyes should be open, interested, and bright. The whites should be clear, with only a few blood vessels visible. There should be no discharge, or excessive accumulation of "matter" in the corners.

- Odor, inflammation, tenderness, or debris in the ears. All of these things are indicative of a parasitic mite infestation that requires treatment by a veterinarian.

- Yellowing of the teeth with pale gums. The discoloration is a sign of built-up plaque, while pale gums can indicate the presence of gum disease or even overall dehydration. Regular dental exams are also important to check for any signs of oral cancer.

Good dental hygiene is fundamental to a cat's overall health. If your pet is agreeable, using a brushing kit on a regular basis is a good idea, as are annual cleanings at the vet's office.

Dental kits that include a brush and feline appropriate toothpaste cost about $7-$10 (£4.60-£6.56) each, while the price of cleanings varies by practice.

As you observe your pet also make sure that:

Chapter 4 – Health Care Facts

- The animal is breathing from the chest, not the abdomen.

- There are no growths, bumps, or masses on the body.

- Litter box use is regular with no "missing," which may indicate an undiagnosed infection.

Egyptian Maus are active, social cats. They love to play and are an involved and vital part of the lives of their humans. If you see any change in your cat's normal behavior, schedule your cat for a checkup. Don't wait and allow a minor, treatable problem to become more serious.

Thankfully, in opting for this breed, you will be selecting one of the most robust of all companion cats. Long life is one of the greatest draws of the Egyptian Mau for the

Chapter 4 – Health Care Facts

potential owner. You will be instantly attached to your Mau and very grateful that he or she will be with you for many years.

Chapter 4 – Health Care Facts

Chapter 5 – Breeding and Showing

Every book on companion breeds like the Egyptian Mau has to talk about breeding and showing at some point, but I don't take the kind of "gung ho" positive approach you will often see in pet books on either topic.

I'm more inclined to emphasize the "nots" of breeding cats.

- Raising pedigreed Egyptian Maus is *not* a hobby.
- Breeding cats is *not* a way to make money.
- Having a cattery is *not* easy, and *not* for everyone.

The only reason to become involved in breeding cats is a true desire to see the genetic quality of the animals promulgated at the highest levels.

Yes, purebred Egyptian Mau kittens sell for high prices, but after all the cattery bills are paid, most breeders are ecstatic to just break even. Being a breeder is about love of the breed. Nothing else.

Deciding to Become a Breeder

While I do actively discourage most people from breeding any type of cat, I do encourage people who *think* they are interested to completely immerse themselves in the cat fancy.

Only when you have experienced the cat culture by attending multiple cat shows and getting to know working breeders can you really judge for yourself.

Chapter 5 – Breeding and Showing

I've already said that attending cat shows is a great way to collect business cards and find breeders from whom to purchase and Egyptian Mau. These are the same people to whom you need to speak – outside the hectic atmosphere of the show itself – if you are considering opening a cattery.

There are also numerous online discussion forums where you can get a feel for the daily ups and downs of cattery life. It's not even necessary to find an Egyptian Mau specific forum.

Any place where breeders gather to talk and share information will give you a sense of what it's like to live with and care for pedigreed animals on a 24/7 basis.

(Any time that you join one of these forums, spend a good period of time, at least a couple of weeks, politely "lurking." Read posts and learn the etiquette of the environment. Don't just dive in and start talking or you may well give offense without realizing what you're doing.)

Factors to Consider

When I say "factors to consider," I don't necessarily mean the mechanics of setting up a cattery. Those things ultimately boil down to process.

These are more the "big questions" that should be carefully and seriously pondered well in advance of any concrete moves to start breeding cats. They involve your lifestyle,

Chapter 5 – Breeding and Showing

environment, support system, and financial situation. All demand that you be honest with yourself.

Can I really commit to caring for the animals?

"Caring" doesn't just mean feeding and watering. Running a cattery is time intensive to the extreme. Your cats will need you day and night. They are no respecters of nights, weekends, or holidays. Your cats will depend on you completely and their needs will dominate your schedule.

Can I stand the losses?

While living your life in the company of beautiful, intelligent cats like Egyptian Maus is a great pleasure, there will be losses of all kinds. Some kittens don't live. Older, beloved cats ultimately pass away. You must send beautiful kittens to new homes.

No matter how much you prepare for each of these events, they all constitute painful losses for people who put their heart and soul into raising and caring for animals.

Do I really have the space?

Obviously, a cattery must be financed, but the issue of adequate room is imperative. If you're keeping a breeding pair, the animals must be separated to prevent unplanned litters.

If you're planning on having the cattery in your home, will you need to add on? How are the neighbors going to react? Are there zoning ordinance or HOA regulations that apply?

Chapter 5 – Breeding and Showing

Will your homeowners insurance cover the facility or do you need a new policy? Find out the answers in advance!

What's your "exit strategy?"

No one likes to go into a new endeavor thinking about failure, but when you operate a cattery you have a responsibility to living creatures in your care.

If your plan fails, can you keep all of your cats? If not, how will they be placed? Do you have enough money to care for them during the time it takes to find good homes?

Running the Numbers

Inherently any estimate of costs is a "best guess" scenario. There are always expenses you will fail to factor into your projections. Each individual cattery faces costs that are unique to the circumstances of location and the wherewithal of the owners.

In "running the numbers" you should at least factor in all of the following items in your calculations:

Reference Materials

Some degree of understanding regarding genetics is necessary in all breeding operations. While you won't be studying for a degree in the subject, you will need to become conversant in the basics of feline genetics in general, and amass as much information as possible on Egyptian Maus in particular.

Chapter 5 – Breeding and Showing

Breeding Pair

It may be impossible for you to afford a breeding pair in the beginning, but you will need a foundation queen or stud. Factor in fees for mating your animals with those from other catteries, including the cost of travel.

Veterinary Services

Your cats will not only need routine veterinary care, but you will also be paying for maternal and infant care, and for repeat testing procedures each time one of your animals visits another cattery for mating. All catteries require FIV/FELV tests prior to pairings.

You must also consider potential emergency scenarios like C-sections for queens, or surgeries and treatments required by specific illnesses including cancers.

Thankfully Egyptian Maus are extremely healthy cats, but you can never rule out unexpected medical needs for any animal.

Furnishing and Toys

This is an area of expense that gets scaled up very easily, especially when you are dealing with active cats like Egyptian Maus that crave intellectual stimulation.

When you are doing your cost estimates, multiple all your projections in this area by the number of cats you anticipate having. These expenses include things like:

- scratching posts
- climbing trees
- beds
- travel crates
- play pens for kittens

And lots and lots of toy!

Construction / Renovation

It's very common for people to add on to or renovate their homes to create an area for their cattery. This could be anything from a room to a wing! You may need the services of an architect, a contractor, or both to use your available space most effectively.

Emergency Reserve

This is that "exit strategy" amount I discussed earlier. All catteries should have an emergency reserve sufficient to cover 3-6 months of expenses in the event that the operation must be shut down and the animals placed in new homes.

Showing Egyptian Maus

Cattery owners become involved in cat shows to publicly display the superiority of their bloodlines. Awards received in exhibition lend prestige to a breeding operation. Showing is therefore a part of animal breeding. It is not, however, a requirement for every owner of a pedigreed Egyptian Mau.

Chapter 5 – Breeding and Showing

The decision to show a cat of any breed should be based on the temperament of the animal and the interest level of the owner. I, personally, have never had a desire to exhibit my animals, although I do enjoy attending cat shows. I have friends who absolutely live for the show ring.

Although Egyptian Maus are gregarious animals that tend to do rather well when shown, even the best socialized of cats doesn't tend to be all that thrilled with the show environment. They certainly don't seem to thrive on it the way dogs do.

If you have a cat that is naturally shy or nervous around strangers, a cat show will be extremely unpleasant for your pet. I don't believe it's fair to put an animal through that for purely human goals.

Chapter 5 – Breeding and Showing

My best advice to you is to go to some shows. Watch what goes on. Learn the ropes – and then decide what's right first for your cat and then for you. Always put the needs and the welfare of the animal first.

That being said, there are some rules and points of order you need to understand even if you are to be nothing more than a spectator at a cat show.

Proper Cat Show Attendance

The primary rule of proper at show attendance is also the one you will find hardest to obey in the beginning. "Don't touch!"

To walk into a venue filled with adorable, high quality pets you cannot touch seems a cruel requirement, but it isn't about you! It's about the cats.

Many feline diseases are so communicable they can be passed from one cat to another through little more than a nose tap. Those same germs can be transferred on your hands.

The "don't touch" rule has one underlying motivation, protecting the cats. If you are asked to pet a cat, the invitation will be proffered with an extended bottle of hand sanitizer. Since you are being granted a rare privilege, say thank you and use the sanitizer!

Chapter 5 – Breeding and Showing

The next major rule also goes against the natural grain, but again, the safety of the cats is the reason for the admonition, "Don't help."

Escapes happen rather often a cat shows and are announced with the cry, "Loose cat." When you hear that alarm raised, stop where you are and don't move or make any noise.

If you see the errant feline, signal the owner and silently indicate the cat's location, but don't try to be a part of the recapture. You'll only scare the cat more and make the situation worse.

Finally, if you hear someone yell, "right of way," move. Cat shows are very hectic. Exhibitors have only a brief amount of time to get to the ring once their names are called. Don't be offended if you're in the middle of a conversation with a breeder only to have the person grab up their cat and dash off.

Respect the pace of the show and understand the need not to hold up a breeder or get in the way of the flow of traffic.

Throughout all of this process, listen to what is going on around you, especially when you are in close proximity to the show ring. This is more than a polite desire not to interrupt the judging. You'll learn a lot from the comments the judge makes while examining the animals.

Chapter 5 – Breeding and Showing

Cat Show Mechanics

Cat shows are an odd mixture of hectic dashes to the ring and glacial periods of waiting. In an effort to enliven the atmosphere and to showcase their cats, exhibitors festively decorate their cats' cages. The animals themselves only leave those cages for actual judging in an effort to mitigate the chance of escapes.

There is a special class reserved specifically for showing household pets, which is a key difference from the dog show world. The pet class is highly popular and is responsible for getting many young people actively interested in the cat fancy.

Pedigreed animals are judged according to breed standards formalized by the various governing bodies of the cat fancy. These include:

- The International Cat Association (TICA)
- Fédération Internationale Féline
- World Cat Federation
- Cat Fanciers Association
- Feline Federation Europe
- Australia Cat Federation
- American Association of Cat Enthusiasts
- American Cat Fanciers Association

The following is the TICA breed standard for the Eyptian Mau to give you an idea of the criteria applied to the breed.

Chapter 5 – Breeding and Showing

Egyptian Mau Breed Standard

HEAD: 35 points

Shape - 4
Ears - 8
Eyes - 15
Muzzle - 4
Profile - 4

BODY: 25 points

Torso - 10
Legs - 5
Feet - 5
Tail - 5

COAT/COLOR/PATTERN: 40 points

Length - 5
Pattern - 20
Color - 15

CATEGORY: Traditional.

DIVISIONS: Tabby and Silver/Smoke.

COLORS: Spotted pattern ONLY, Bronze spotted tabby, Black Silver spotted tabby, and Black Smoke ONLY.

PERMISSIBLE OUTCROSSES: None.

Chapter 5 – Breeding and Showing

HEAD:

Shape: Medium length, slightly modified wedge without flat planes. Cheeks are not full.

Ears: Medium to medium large, moderately pointed, broad at base. Upstanding with ample width between ears, set well back on head, cupped forward, alert. Short, close lying hair on outside, may have lynx tips.

Eyes: Large, rounded almond shape. Aperture is level in head with slight upward slant to lower lid. Neither round nor oriental. Gooseberry green (light green). Allowance is made for changing eye color, with some discernable green by 8 months of age and full green eye color by 18 months of age. Preference given at all ages for greener eyes.

Muzzle: Medium-rounded, neither short nor pointed, rounded planes blending with overall head shape. Allow for jowls in mature males.
Nose: Even in width throughout length.

Profile: Gentle rise from bridge of nose to forehead, which then flows into arched neck without a break.

BODY:

Torso: Balanced between cobby and foreign types. Medium in size, medium-long length. The shoulder blades are high and angulated. There is a loose skin flap (belly flap).

Legs: Medium in length, with hind legs proportionately longer. Medium boning with well-developed musculature. The hind legs are longer than the front, but carried flexed so the back is level.

Feet: Slightly oval, almost round. Small in size, with very long toes on back feet.

Tail: Medium length, medium at with slight taper.

Boning: Medium.

Musculature: Well-developed.

COAT/COLOR:

Length: Medium, long enough to carry two bands of ticking.

Texture: Bronze and Black Silver - resilient, close-lying. Black Smoke - fine, silky, close-lying.

PATTERN: There is good contrast between pale ground color and deeper markings. The forehead has characteristic tabby "M" and frown lines, which run between the ears and down the back of the neck, becoming elongated spots along the spine. On the haunches the spine lines meld into a dorsal stripe, which continues to the tip of the tail. The tail is banded with the tip dark.

The cheeks have mascara lines, from the corner of the eye along the contour of the cheek, with the second line starting at the center of the cheek and curving upward, almost meeting the first line below the ear. There are one or more necklaces, broken in the center.

The shoulder markings are a transition between stripes and spots. The upper legs are heavily barred but do not necessarily match. The spots on the body are random, with variance in size and shape. The pattern on the sides of the body may be unmatched, but spots should not form a broken mackerel pattern. The haunches and thighs have stripes, which break into elongated spots on the lower leg. Belly spots should have good contrast against pale ground color.

COLORS:

Black Silver: Markings are charcoal to black with good contrast. Back of ears grayish-pink tipped with black. Upper throat, chin and nostrils silver, appearing white.
Bronze: Color darkest on saddle, fading to tawny buff on sides and creamy ivory on undersides. Back of ears tawny pink tipped in dark brown. Bridge of nose ocherous. Upper throat, chin and nostrils pale, creamy white.

Black Smoke: Charcoal gray to black with silver undercolor with no ticking. All markings jet black with enough contrast to make a well-defined pattern plainly visible.

GENERAL DESCRIPTION: The Egyptian Mau is the only natural domestic breed of spotted cat. The body is graceful, showing well-developed muscular strength. It strikes a balance between the heftiness of the cobby and svelteness of the oriental types. It is an alert, active, strong, colorful cat of medium size. It should be well-balanced physically and temperamentally. General balance is more to be desired than size alone.

ALLOWANCES: Broad head and jowls in mature males. Very muscular necks and shoulders in mature males.

PENALIZE: Lack of green ring in eye color of cats over the age of 7 months and amber cast in eye color in cats over the age of 1.5 years. Short or round head; pointed muzzle; full cheeks, small ears; small, round or oriental eyes; cobby or oriental body, short or whippy tail; spots on body which run together; unbroken necklaces; poor condition.

WITHHOLD ALL AWARDS (WW): Lack of spots; wrong eye color; white locket or spots; lack of ticking in silver or bronze; ticking in smoke; red coloring in bronze. Lack of gray undercoat in bronze. Glitter, rosettes, pelt-like coat.

Chapter 6 – Egyptian Mau Cat Breeders

Austria

ISISKA Egyptian Maus
Vienna, Austria
Phone: 0043 171 70776 60970043 171 70776 6097
Phone: 0776 778 34500776 778 3450
Email: isiska-egyptian-maus@hotmail.com
www.isiska.co.uk

Canada

Chapter 6 – Egyptian Mau Cat Breeders

British Columbia

Azshara Egyptian Maus
Email: azsharamaus@gmail.com
Phone: 250-724-3420
www.azsharamaus.com

New Brunswick

Maus'Art Egyptian Maus
Email: juliecarrier4@hotmail.com
www.mausart.com

Ontario

Jewels Nile Egyptian Maus
Email: jewelsnile@live.com
Cell Phone: 416-910-6831
www.jewelsnile.net

Finland

FIN*Staruskan Egyptian Maus
hannele.arantola@elisanet.fi
Phone: +35840 745 83 15
kationi.wix.com/staruskan#!

France

Amiel-Goshen
Normandy, France
Home +33 (0) 214 402 641+33 (0) 214 402 641 or
Mobile +33 (0) 630 862 352+33 (0) 630 862 352

Chapter 6 – Egyptian Mau Cat Breeders

patrick@monacocattery.com
www.monacocattery.com

Grande Pyramide
Hauts de Seine - 92
France
Mobile : +33 (0)6 65 27 07 63+33 (0)6 65 27 07 63
www.chatteriegrandepyramide.com

Le Fort de la Bosse Marniere
Limetz-Villez, Île-de-France region in north-central France.
Phone: +33 (0) 1 30 93 06 49+33 (0) 1 30 93 06 49
Email: bernard.boucher.svs@wanadoo.fr
www.labossemarniere.com

Ireland

Acclaim Egyptian Maus
Northern Ireland
Phone: 02893382185 or 07886739683
Email: thecatsalley@aol.com

Italy

Aequinoctium Cattery
Brescia (northern Italy near Milano)
Scaglia Marco
Phone: +39 339 8488091+39 339 8488091
Email: marco72xyz@libero.it
www.aequinoctium.it

Chapter 6 – Egyptian Mau Cat Breeders

Netherlands

Cattery-Obsidiaan
Emmen, Netherlands
Phone: +31-(0)591-659067+31-(0)591-659067
Email: h.j.feenstra@cattery-obsidiaan.com
www.cattery-obsidiaan.com

Scotland

Mintander Egyptian Maus
Rosyth, Fife.
Phone: 01383 41442101383 414421 or 07517 48885607517 488856
Email: isabelkita@msn.com

Saqqara Egyptian Maus
East Kilbride, West Scotland
Phone: 01355 26094201355 260942
Email: gillybeen@hotmail.co.uk
www.saqqaraegyptianmaus.co.uk

Weesams Egyptian Maus
Scotland
Phone: 01542 81025301542 810253
Email: weesams@btinternet.com
www.freewebs.com/weesamscats

Chapter 6 – Egyptian Mau Cat Breeders

United Kingdom

Aanisis Egyptian Maus
Tyne & Wear
Phone: 0191 584 58940191 584 5894
Email: anna@aanisis.co.uk
www.aanisis.co.uk

Accio Egyptian Maus
Gillingham, Kent
Phone: 01634 26857901634 268579
Email: keeble76@btinternet.com
www.accioegyptianmaus.co.uk

Amorcatz
Evesham, Worcestershire
Phone: 01386 4569501386 45695 or 07791 10337807791 103378
Email: sueamor@aol.com

Ashidah Egyptian Maus
Essex
Phone: 01206 21065101206 210651
Email: jacana66@talktalk.net

Autari Egyptian Maus
Nottingham
Phone: 07909 65206007909 652060
Email: anthonylane@autarimaus.com
www.autarimaus.com

Chapter 6 – Egyptian Mau Cat Breeders

Aysifa Egyptian Maus
Phone: 07932 65336507932 653365
Email: info@aysifa.co.uk
www.Aysifa.co.uk

Bastetetra Egyptian Maus
St Albans
Phone: 01582 76981001582 769810
Email: jeanie_hunt@hotmail.com

Geniemau Egyptian Maus
County Durham
Phone: 0191 37127290191 3712729
Phone: 07712 80501007712 805010
Email: geanielamb@talktalk.net
www.geniemau.com

Hapimaus
Wiltshire
Phone: 01793 77182701793 771827
Mobile: 07460 60700707460 607007
Email: jansmaus@hotmail.co.uk

Mauology
Tyne & Wear
Phone: 0191 385 79840191 385 7984
Email: mauology@talktalk.net
mauology.com

Chapter 6 – Egyptian Mau Cat Breeders

Memphis Maus
Bromley, Kent
Phone: 020 8313 1712020 8313 1712 (Home)
Phone: 077 66 735 456077 66 735 456 (Mobile)
Email: clive@memphismaus.co.uk
www.memphismaus.co.uk

Mustafa Mau
Ipswich
Phone: 07780 53534807780 535348
Email: mustafamaulouise@aol.co.uk
www.mustafamau.co.uk

Newkingdom Egyptian Maus
Tyne & Wear
Phone: 0191 23319740191 2331974
Email: Melissa.Bateson@ncl.ac.uk
www.geocities.com/new_kingdom.geo

Sinaicats
Shropshire
Phone: 01743 741611 or 07870572160
Email: sinaicats@live.com
www.sinaicats.co.uk

Starrsailor Egyptian Maus
West Yorkshire
Phone: 01924 46627401924 466274
Email: starrsailor06@yahoo.co.uk
www.starrsailormaus.co.uk

Chapter 6 – Egyptian Mau Cat Breeders

Starshadow Egyptian Maus
Lincolnshire
Phone: 01476 86102201476 861022
Email: michele.dirhams@hotmail.co.uk

Tarjjika Egyptian Maus
Andover, Hampshire
Phone: 01264 31308501264 313085
Email: liz_case1@hotmail.com
www.tarjjika.info

Thizaloe Egyptian Maus
Ashford, Kent
Phone: 01233 62427901233 624279
Email: steve.murton@ntlworld.com
www.thizalowe.co.uk

Tiggermau Egyptian Maus
Washington, Tyne & Wear
Phone: 0191 43199690191 4319969
Email: Yvonnemau2@virginmedia.com
www.tiggermau.co.uk

Whitecrest Egyptian Maus
West Midlands
Phone: 0121 557 20350121 557 2035 or 01922 44882501922 448825
Email: j.whitehouse1@ssesurf.co.uk or kinstone@blueyonder.co.uk

Chapter 6 – Egyptian Mau Cat Breeders

United States

California

Platinum Maus Egyptian Maus
Email: platinummaus@gmail.com
Phone: 619-397-1926
www.platinummaus.com

Royalnefertt Egyptian Maus
Email: nefertiti-maus@sbcglobal.net
Phone: 714-504-7079
www.nefertitimaus.com

Connecticut

Mt. Sinai Egyptian Maus
Email: mt.sinaicattery@yahoo.com
mt.sinaicattery.tripod.com

District of Columbia

Emauge Egyptian
Email: emaugedc@yahoo.com
Phone: 202-543-2733

Florida

Maullenium Egyptian Maus
Email: DMard@aol.com
www.maullenium.com

Chapter 6 – Egyptian Mau Cat Breeders

Mas-Ree Mau Egyptian Maus
Email: EgyptMau@aol.com
Phone: 904-757-9469
www.masreemaus.com

Kansas

Touch O Katz Egyptian Maus
Email: kspersian@yahoo.com
www.touchokatz.webs.com

Kitkatkorner Egyptian Maus
Email: goodelll@ckt.net
Phone: 620-852-3385 (evening)
fizzer77.tripod.com

Cattitude Egyptian Maus
Email: catswithcattitude@yahoo.com
Phone: 316-772-2243
Cell Phone: 620-947-2243
www.catswithcattitude.com

Maine

KarMau Egyptian Maus
Email: ramblek@maine.rr.com
Phone: 207-468-6755
www.karmau-cats.com

Chapter 6 – Egyptian Mau Cat Breeders

Maryland
Mautrix Egyptian Maus
Email: mautrixcats@aol.com
Phone: 410-825-9824

Michigan

Ajatarah Egyptian Maus
Email: maugirl734@yahoo.com
www.ajatarah.com

New York

Marzac Knoll Egyptian Maus
Email: egeorge2@rochester.rr.com
Phone: 585-394-8728
www.spotsgalore.com

Ohio

Aar-gee Em Egyptian Maus
Email: maus@aargeeem.com
Phone: 440-238-1491
aargeeem.com

Oregon

Ramah Egyptian Maus
Email: dee@ramahmaus.com
Phone: 541-899-1234
Fax: 541-899-2027
www.ramahmaus.com

Pennsylvania

Azulencos Egyptian Maus
Email: azulencosnoblecats@gmail.com
www.facebook.com/azulencos

Texas

Khemenu Egyptian Maus
Email: khemenu_cats@yahoo.com
Phone: 972-408-6090
www.khemenucattery.com

Virginia

Emau Egyptian Maus
Email: emau@louisa.net
Phone: 540-967-0495
www.emaucats.com

Washington (State)

Kirydashi Egyptian Maus
Email: m4bigsky@yahoo.com
Phone: 253-653-1572
www.kirydashi.com

Wisconsin

Amaure Egyptian Maus
Email: mau.catlover@yahoo.com
www.amaure.webs.com

Afterword

I hope you've enjoyed learning more about Egyptian Mau cats in particular and feline husbandry in general. I've had cats all of my life, since childhood, and have a deep set love for many different breeds including the common "alley cat." All are fascinating creatures, but I have to confess, I think the Egyptian Mau is an exception among exceptions.

Heidi is unlike any cat I've ever had and she is a pure joy to have in the house. She is my beloved friend and companion. I cherish her boundless enthusiasm for life, deep affection for my family, and her bright, inquisitive mind.

Through Heidi, I have come to greatly admire the Egyptian Mau breed. I personally think there is no better companion animal, but I am always quick to add that your Mau will need your time, attention, and interaction.

They don't lose their mind with separation anxiety the way a Siamese will, but they do expect you to be home on time, prepared to give a full report on your day and to hear their remarks on what they did while you were at work.

I don't always completely understand what Heidi is trying to tell me, but I listen attentively all the same. I really don't have a choice. She's been known to reach out with her paw and pull me back into the conversation!

As one of the oldest of all breeds, it almost seems as if the Egyptian Mau has spent centuries perfecting themselves to

Afterword

represent the best of what it means to be feline. I have seen statues of the goddess Bastet on display in museums and been struck by how the profile is so exactly the lovely form of my own pet.

From the days of the ancient Egyptians to the present the "wild" appearing, but thoroughly domesticated spotted Mau has remained a thoroughly regal presence in the cat world.

Relevant Websites

Breed Profile: The Egyptian Mau
The Cat Fanciers' Association
www.cfa.org/client/breedEgyptianMau.aspx

TICA Egyptian Mau Breed Introduction
www.tica.org/public/breeds/em/intro.php

Egyptian Mau Rescue Organization
www.emaurescue.org

Global Egyptian Mau Society
www.egyptianmau.org

Association Internationale du Mau Egyptien
www.aime.us/AIME_us.htm

The Egyptian Mau Club
www.egyptianmaus.co.uk

Egyptian Mau Breed Synopsis
American Cat Fanciers Association
www.acfacat.com/egyptian_mau_synopsis.htm

CFA Egyptian Mau Breed Council
www.egyptianmaubc.org

The Egyptian Mau Cat
The Governing Council of the Cat Fancy
www.gccfcats.org/breeds/mau.html

Relevant Websites

The Egyptian Mau Cat Club of Australasia
aussie-maus.tripod.com/home.htm

Cats 101: Egyptian Mau
Video: Animal Planet
www.animalplanet.com/tv-shows/cats-101/videos/egyptian-mau.htm

Egyptian Mau Cat Breed Information
Vetstreet
www.vetstreet.com/cats/egyptian-mau

Frequently Asked Questions

Although I recommend you read the entire text to really understand how to select and care for your Egyptian Mau, the following are some of the most commonly asked questions about this exquisite breed.

Do Egyptian Maus cats actually come from Egypt?

The first three Egyptian Maus to appear in the United States were imported from Egypt via Italy by a Russian princess, Nathalie Troubetskoy – an appropriately regal story for these very royal cats.

Troubetskoy founded a cattery and the cats she raised are now considered the traditional Egyptian Mau lines.

What are the accepted colorations for the Mau?

Egyptian Maus have short, silky coats that are naturally spotted. The accepted colors are silver, smoke, bronze, black and their dilutes (blue silver, blue spotted, blue smoke, and blue.) Black and dilute Egyptian Maus are not shown.

A Mau's spots cannot run together, but must be clearly visible. They can be of any size or shape. The spine should be highlighted by a dark, dorsal stripe running from the head to the tail.

Frequently Asked Questions

Are Egyptian Maus large cats?

The Egyptian Mau is classified as a medium sized cat. They range in size from 6 lbs. to 14 lbs. /2.72 kg to 6.35 kg.

Females average 6 lbs. to 8 lbs. / 2.72 kg to 3.62 kg and males 7 lbs. and 14 lbs / 3.17 kg to 6.35 kg.

Does the Egyptain Mau have any wild blood?

The Egyptian Mau is a completely domesticated cat with no wild blood.

Does the Egyptian Mau have a good temperament?

The Mau is an extremely people oriented and interactive act. They do well with other animals and love to be a part of everything that is going on, following their humans around the house and often riding on their shoulders or settling in their laps.

Although shy around strangers, the Egyptian Mau bonds strongly with its owners, playfully inventing games, retrieving toys, and expertly exploring every nook and cranny of the house. Their cleverness and devoted good humor makes them delightful companions.

Does the Egyptian Mau have any special requirements?

The Egyptian Mau does not have any special needs or requirements, but as with all companion breeds, especially those with a "wild" appearance, they should be kept strictly indoors for their own safety.

They especially enjoy watching and chattering at birds, so a window perch will be much appreciated, as will a nice scratching post.

Do not allow your Mau to free feed. The breed is very prone to putting on weight, and they are highly diet resistant, preferring to go on a protracted hunger strike until they get the food they want, in the quantities they want.

Is the Egyptian Mau a vocal breed?

Egyptian Maus do love to talk, but they don't have the strident and insistent voices characteristic of other oriental breeds, in particular the Siamese. A Mau's voice is melodious and gentle, more giving to chirping and chortling than outright mewing.

A female Mau in season can literally raise the roof, but since pet quality adoptions from reputable catteries require that females be spayed, this isn't a problem with which most owners will have to cope.

At what age should spaying or neutering be performed?

For both genders the surgeries to spay or neuter should be performed before the kitten reaches six months of age.

Frequently Asked Questions

Is there any temperament difference between males and females?

Although the gender question comes up constantly, I think it is, for the most part, a complete misconception that cats of any breed are "better" in one or the other gender.

Every cat is an individual in his or her own right and will behave much more in accordance with its life experience than with any innate gender traits.

The dominant fear is, of course, that males will spray, but this behavior is very rare in neutered animals. In more than 40 years of cat ownership I have never had a male cat spray in the house.

Males of almost all breeds tend to be larger, but there are no appreciable differences in temperament between genders, and certainly not with Egyptian Mau toms and queens.

Does the Egyptian Mau get along well with children?

This is another question to which I give a fairly standard answer. All cats will get along well with well-behaved children who have been taught to respect and be kind to animals.

Maus are very playful, but they won't tolerate being teased or mistreated. In most instances they will simply absent themselves, but any animal that is in pain or is afraid will react according to its instincts.

Frequently Asked Questions

In almost all cases, however, I believe you have to ask who is really to blame for the encounter, the cat or the child? If your children are not well behaved around animals, you should not have pets until the child is prepared to behave responsibly and appropriately.

Do Egyptian Maus get along well with other pets?

Egyptian Maus do fine in the company of other animals when the introductions are made early in life and the other pets are well behaved and congenial.

Older Maus have already developed their preferences and attachments and can be highly territorial, making new additions to the family not impossible, but certainly more challenging.

How much does an Egyptian Mau cost?

For a pet quality Egyptian Mau, prices range from $585-$750 / £350-£450. Show quality females are $1000+ / £600+ while males are often sold for more than $1675+ / £1000+.

(Prices vary widely by breeder, location, age, and bloodline.)

Frequently Asked Questions

Glossary

A

Ailurophile - A person who loves cats.

Ailurophobe - A person who fears or even hates cat.

Allergen - In relation to cats, the primary allergen, the substance that causes an allergic reaction in some people, is, Fel d 1, a protein produced by the cat's sebaceous glands, and present in its saliva.

Allergy - A high level of sensitivity present in some people to a given substance, like the protein Fel d 1 in cats. Generally the reaction includes, but is not limited to watering eyes, sneezing, itching, and skin rashes.

Alter - A term that refers to the neutering or spaying of a cat or dog.

B

Bloodline - The verifiable line of descent that establishes an animal's pedigree.

Breed Standard - A set of standards for a given breed formulated by parent breed clubs and used as the basis for evaluating show quality animals.

Glossary

Breed - Term that refers to a group of cats with defined physical characteristics that are related by common ancestry.

Breeder - A person who works with a particular breed of cats, producing offspring from high-quality dams and sires for the purpose of maintaining and improving the genetic quality of the line.

Breeding - The process in which dams and sires are paired for the purpose of producing offspring.

Breeding Program - An organized and ongoing program in which cats are mated selectively to produce offspring that are ideal examples of the breed.

Breeding Quality - A term describing a cat that meets the standards of a given breed to a degree sufficient to be included in a breeding program.

Breed True - The phrase that describes the capacity of a male and female cat to produce kittens that closely resemble themselves in accepted elements of the breed standard.

C

Carpal Pads - Located on a cat's front legs at the "wrists," these pads provide added traction for the animal's gait.

Castrate - The medical procedure whereby a male cat's testicles are removed.

Glossary

Caterwaul - A feline vocalization that produces a discordant, shrill sound.

Cat Fancy - Term used to describe the overall group of registered associations clubs, and individuals that breed and show cats.

Catnip - A member of the mint family, this aromatic perennial herb (*Nepeta cataria*) contains an oil to which some cats are strongly attracted and to which they respond with a kind of "stoned" intoxication. Kittens cannot respond to catnip until they are 8-9 months of age.

Cattery - Any establishment that exists for the purpose of housing cats, and where they are bred as part of an organized program.

Certified Pedigree - A pedigree that has been issued in an official capacity by a feline registering association.

Clowder - A collective term for a group of cats.

Coat - Term referring to a cat's fur.

Crate - Container used to safely transport cats from one location to another or to confine them temporarily for their own safety.

Crepuscular - Although known in popular lore as nocturnal animals, cats are actually crepuscular, meaning they are most active at dusk and dawn.

Glossary

Crossbred - A cat that is the product of breeding a sire and a dam of different breeds.

D

Dam - The female in a parenting set of cats.

Dander - The small scale of hair and skin that are shed by an animal. Often responsible for allergic reactions in individuals with a sensitivity to the substance.

Declawing - A highly controversial surgical procedure that removes a cat's claws permanently.

Desex - Describes the alteration of an animal by neutering or spaying.

Domesticated - Animals that have been tamed to live with or work with humans, or that have chosen to cultivate such a relationship.

E

Ear Mites - Microscopic parasites that feed on the lining of a cat's ear canal, causing debris to build up, generating a foul odor, and resulting in extreme itching.

Entire - A term describing a cat that has an intact reproductive system.

Exhibitor - An individual that participates in organized cat shows.

Glossary

F

Fel d 1 - A protein produced by the cat's sebaceous glands, and present in its saliva, which causes an allergic reaction in some people.

Feline - A member of the family Felidae. Includes lions, tigers, jaguars, and wild and domestic cats.

Fleas - Various bloodsucking insects of the order *Siphonaptera*. They are wingless, and their legs are adapted for jumping. They are parasitical, and feed off warm-blooded animals.

Flehmening/Flehmen Reaction - A facial gesture in cats that is often mistaken for a grimace. In reality, the cat is drawing in air to pass it over a special structure in the roof of the mouth called the Jacobsen's Organ, which functions as a second set of nostrils and allows cats to "taste" a scent.

G

Gene pool - In a population of organisms, the "gene pool" is the collective genetic information relative to reproduction.

Genes - Determine particular characteristics in a given organism. They are a distinct hereditary unit and consist of a DNA sequence occupying a specific location on a chromosome.

Glossary

Genetic - Refers to any trait, characteristic, tendency, or condition that is inherited.

Genetically Linked Defects - Health specific problems or those relative to temperament that are passed from one generation to the next.

Genetics - The scientific study of heredity.

Genotype - Refers to the genetic makeup of an organism or a group of organisms.

Groom - The act of caring for the coat of a feline, which may include brushing, combing, trimming, or washing.

Guard Hair - Long, coarse hairs that form the outer layer of a cat's coat.

H

Heat - The seasonal estrus cycle of a female cat (or any other mammal).

Hereditary - Any characteristic, trait, disease, or condition that can be genetically transmitted from parent to offspring.

Histamine - A physiologically active amine in plant and animal tissue released from mast cells as part of an allergic reaction in humans.

Hock - Anatomical term describing the ankle of a cat's hind leg.

Glossary

Household Pet - A cat not registered to be exhibited or shown in competition.

Housetraining - The process whereby a cat is trained to use a litter box to live cleanly in a house.

Humane Societies - Any one of a number of groups that work to put an end to animal suffering due to overt acts of cruelty and other impoverishing or harmful circumstances.

I

Immunization - The use of inoculations to create immunity against disease. Also referred to as vaccination.

Innate - A quality, trait, or tendency present at birth and thus inborn

Inbreeding - When two closely-related cats of the same breed are mated.

Instinct - A pattern of behavior in a species that is inborn and comes in response to specific environmental stimuli.

Intact - Animals that are intact possess their complete reproductive system. They have not been neutered or spayed.

J

Jacobsen's Organ - An organ located in the roof of a cat's mouth that allows it to "taste" a scent. Appears as two small openings and is regarded as a second set of "nostrils."

Glossary

K

Kindle - A collective term for a group of kittens. An alternate term is "chowder."

Kitten - Young cats under the age of 6 months.

L

Lactation - Process by which the mammary glands form and secrete milk.

Lactating - Term used for a mammalian mother when she is secreting or producing milk.

Litter - The number of offspring in a single birth. Generally 3-4 in cats, although 6-10 is not uncommon.

Litter Box - A container filled with commercial kitty litter or sand and used in the home as a sanitary and manageable location for a cat to urinate and defecate.

M

Mites - Small arachnids (of the order Acarina) that are parasites on animals and plants. Often seen in the ears of felines.

Moggy - The term for a mixed breed cat in the United Kingdom.

Glossary

Muzzle - In cats, the part of the head projecting forward including the mouth, nose, and jaws. May also be referred to as the snout.

N

Neuter - The term used to describe castrating a male cat.

Nictitating Membrane - A cat's third eyelid, which is a transparent inner eyelid that serves to protect and moisten the eye.

Nocturnal - Term used to describe animals that are most active at night. It is mistakenly applied to cats, who are actually crepuscular, being most active at dawn and dusk.

P

Papers - The documentation of a cat's pedigree and registration.

Pedigree - A cat's genealogy presented in writing and spanning three or more generations.

Pet Quality - A cat that does not sufficiently meet the accepted standard for its breed to be shown in competition or to be used in a breeding program.

Q

Queen - An intact female cat, one that has not been spayed.

Glossary

Quick - The vascular portion of a cat's claw that will, if clipped, bleed profusely.

R

Rabies - A viral disease that is highly infections and typically fatal to warm blooded animals. It attacks the central nervous system and is transmitted by the bite of an infected animal.

Recognition - The point at which a cat breed is officially accepted under a cat fancy organization's rules.

Registered Cat - A cat registered through a recognized feline association that has documentation of its ancestry.

Registered Name - The official name used by a registered cat, which is typically long and reflective of its ancestry.

Registration - The record of the particulars of a cat's birth and ancestry filed with an official organization.

Scratching Post - A tower-like structure covered in carpet or rope that allows a cat to sharpen and clean its claws inside the house without being destructive to furniture.

S

Shelter - Any local organization that exists for the purpose of rescuing and caring for homeless and stray animals. Also works to find permanent homes for these animals.

Glossary

Show - An organized exhibition in which judges evaluate cats according to accepted standard for each breed and make awards accordingly.

Show Cat - Cats that participate in shows.

Show Quality - Cats that meet the standards for their breed at a sufficient level to compete in organized cat shows.

Show Standard - A description of the ideal qualities of a breed of cats used as the basis for which the cats are judged in competition. Also known as standard of point.

Sire - The male member of a parenting set of cats.

Spay - The surgery to remove a female cat's ovaries.

Spray - A territorial behavior typically seen in male cats whereby the animal emits a stream of urine as a marker.

Stud - An intact male cat that has not been altered and is used as part of a breeding program.

Subcutaneous - Placed just below the skin, as in an injection.

T

Tapetum Lucidum - The interior portion of a cat's eye that aids in night vision and is highly reflective.

Glossary

V

Vaccine - A weakened or dead preparation of a bacterium, virus, or other pathogen used to stimulate the production of antibodies for the purpose of creating immunity against the disease when injected.

W

Wean - The point at which a kitten begins to eat solid food and is taken off its mother's milk as the primary source of nutrition.

Whisker Break - Refers to an indentation of the upper jaw on a cat.

Whisker Pad - The thickened or fatty pads on either side of a cat's face holding rows of sensory whiskers.

Whole - A cat of either gender that is intact, and has not been neutered or spayed.

Index

adoption, 31, 32, 33, 34, 36, 38, 39
African Serval, 15
air fresheners, 60, 61
American Association of Cat Enthusiasts, 88
Australia Cat Federation, 88
autism, 70
beds, 84
behaviors, 21
Bengal, 20, 29
bloodline, 39, 43, 113
boredom, 46
bowl, 2, 23, 40, 48, 49, 53, 55
breeders, 26, 29, 30, 32, 33, 79, 80
Breeding, 79, 116
breeding pair, 81, 83
brushing, 120
calicivirus, 72
canned food, 49
cardiomyopathy, 67
carnivores, 49, 53
Cat Fancier's Association, 26
catteries, 34, 37, 69, 83, 84, 111
cattery, 83
Cesar Millan, 72
Chausie, 15
children, 24, 70, 112, 113
Chlamydophilia, 72
chocolate, 51
claw clipping, 39
claws, 118, 124
climbing trees, 84
clumping litters, 58
conjunctivitis, 72
costs, 30, 43, 55, 82
dampness, 60
dehydration, 52, 75
dental exams, 75
dental hygiene, 75
dewormed, 34
diet, 40, 49, 50, 53, 111
disease, 120, 121, 124, 126
Distemper Combo, 71
ears, 14, 18, 19, 37, 48, 75, 90, 91, 92, 93, 122
Egyptian Mau, 1, 13, 14, 16, 17, 20, 21, 24, 25, 26, 27, 29, 30, 31, 33, 36, 40, 43, 45, 46, 47, 49, 53, 54, 62, 63, 64, 65, 67, 74, 76, 79, 80, 84, 89, 92, 93, 105, 109, 110, 111, 112, 113
Egyptian Mau Rescue Organization (EMRO), 26
Europe, 38, 88

Index

eyes, 17, 19, 37, 72, 75, 90, 93, 115
F1, 15
F3, 15
F4, 15
fecal parasites, 38
Fédération Internationale Féline, 88
Feline Leukemia, 72
FELV/FIV, 38
fleas, 37
food, 40, 48, 49, 50, 51, 53, 54, 55, 56, 111, 126
gastrointestinal, 42, 52
genetic conditions, 39
gestation period, 20
grooming, 38, 41
gums, 75
head, 18, 19, 90, 93, 109, 123
health evaluations, 39
hearing, 48
houseplants, 42
infectious diseases, 70
joint pain, 74
kitten, 34, 126
kittens, 20, 21, 30, 34, 35, 36, 40, 41, 79, 81, 84, 116, 122
litter, 29, 35, 40, 49, 56, 57, 58, 59, 60, 61, 121, 122
litter box, 121

male, 16, 22, 25, 112, 116, 123, 125
mat, 58, 60
methylxanthines, 51
milk, 52, 122, 126
neuter, 68, 111
odor, 49, 57, 58, 60, 118
offspring, 39, 116, 120, 122
oral cancer, 75
panleukopenia, 72
pedigreed, 29, 30, 32, 33, 38, 68, 79, 80, 84
pets, 23, 25, 32, 36, 42, 43, 67, 71, 86, 88, 113
plant-based materials, 59
plaque, 75
play pens, 84
protein, 49, 115, 119
Rabies, 72, 124
rescue, 27, 43
respiratory infection, 37
rhinotracheitis, 72
Russian Blue, 46
Safari, 16
Savannah, 14
scattering, 60
scratching posts, 39, 84
screen, 60
sensory, 47, 126
separation anxiety, 45, 105
Serengeti, 15, 16
show, 115, 117

Index

showing, 47, 79, 88, 92
Silica gel, 60
sniffing, 43
socialization, 23, 35, 36
spay, 68, 111
stroke, 71
teeth, 75
The Egyptian Mau Breeders and Fanciers Club, 26
The Egyptian Mau Club, 26
The International Cat Association, 15
The International Egyptian Mau Society, 26
TICA breed standard, 88
toxic, 42, 51
toys, 36, 83
training, 39, 62, 63, 64
travel crates, 84
trees, 39, 84
United States, 14, 38, 101, 109
vaccinations, 34, 70, 71
veterinarian, 32, 54, 67, 70, 71, 75
water, 2, 23, 47, 52, 54, 56
weight, 17, 25, 50, 74, 111
whisker stress, 55
wiggle tail, 21, 25
xylitol, 51

www.ingramcontent.com/pod-product-compliance
Lightning Source LLC
LaVergne TN
LVHW051841080426
835512LV00018B/2995